Pooches and Small Fry

Parenting in the 90s

by Jack and Colleen McDaniel

Doral Publishing, Inc.
Wilsonville, Oregon
1995

Published by Doral Publishing, Inc., 8560 SW Salish Ln #300, Wilsonville OR 97070-9612. Order through Login Publishers Consortium, Chicago IL

Printed in the United States of America.

Edited by Luana Luther.
Cover design by Pam Posey.
Drawings by Lon Walker.

Library of Congress Number: 94-69540
ISBN: 0-944875-37-8

McDaniel, Jack.
    Pooches and small fry : parenting in the
90s / by Jack and Colleen McDaniel. --
Wilsonville, Or. : Doral Pub., 1995.   •

    p. : ill. ; cm.
    Includes index.

    1. Dogs--Behavior. 2. Dogs--Psychology.
3. Dogs--Training.   I. McDaniel, Colleen.
II. Title.

SF433.M   636.7 dc20
                    00-

*to the thousands of dogs and clients
who have been willing to share their lives with us...
we couldn't have done it without you.*

Acknowledgements

To Jaye Lane: You grabbed our dream and gave it substance. To Greg Smith: You took the substance and gave it life; we truly can not thank you enough. To Luana Luther: You took that life and delivered it into existence. Thank you.

To Nancy Baer: Your dedication and encouragement and just plain hard work often provided that much-needed light at the end of a sometimes long tunnel.

And, finally, to Chaos: An Irish Water Spaniel who had her own way of looking at the world; and she decided her world needed to include both Jack and Colleen. Thank you.

Table of Contents

Part I. Learning & Perception

Introduction 3

Chapter 1.Pack Theory 9

Chapter 2.Developmental Timelines 17

Part II. Communication & Education

Introduction 33

Chapter 3.Becoming Alpha and Staying That Way 35

Chapter 4.Building a Foundation 51

Chapter 5.Training Through Leadership 65

Part III. Behavior & Behaviorism

Introduction 105

Chapter 6.Behavior & Pack Dynamics 109

Chapter 7.Unconscious Reinforcement of Negative Behavior 119

Chapter 8.Physiology & Behavior 141

Part IV. The Joys of Parenting

Chapter 9.Are You Ready for This? 151

Chapter 10.Encouraging Words 165

Part V

Index 169

Part I
Learning & Perception

Introduction

There are many books in the stores these days that tell you how to train your dog. This isn't one of them. Instead, this book is about behavior, particularly the similarities between canine and human learning behaviors, and how to understand and influence them.

It may seem a bit odd at first to think that canines and people share any behaviors at all, even very general ones, let alone something as important as learning the things that shape attitudes and behavior. Even so, all animals exhibit both instinctive and learned behaviors. In short, all animals have the capacity to learn things, and so it shouldn't be too surprising that many species go about learning in similar ways. And, since people are animals too, it follows that they, too, have something in common with how other animals go about learning.

The similarities between how people and other animals learn are much more common and specific than you might think, particularly between people and dogs. Dogs and people have been together for a long time, probably since people first started to live together in groups. We've hunted together, eaten the same food and slept in the same camps for a long, long time—we still do—but our similarities are much more significant than just doing things together. We actually think much the same way about certain things as do dogs, and we are influenced by what we're taught by our parents and our teachers in the same way dogs are influenced by their parents and teachers. As an example of our similarities in perception, consider that both an adult dog and a two-year-old child have roughly the same limited understanding of abstract ideas. That is, the two-year old is about as likely to grasp the notion of money, time and ethics as is your dog. As a result, the ways that we go about teaching both the dog and the two-year old have much in common: We're going to put ourselves in their shoes to see how they understand things so we can educate them, and we're also going to have to be aware of their limitations in learning, even though they're both quite capable of learning a great deal.

The resemblance gets even more striking. Even as the human child grows older, some of the similarities between human and canine learning processes continue to be shared. Naturally, as the human grows older his reasoning capacity far outstrips that of the dog. Even so, many of the developmental learning stages and processes between people and dogs remain alike as each progresses from childhood to adolescence to adulthood to old age. What we and dogs learn early on in our lives has a lasting impact on our behaviors and attitudes forever after; and, these behaviors and attitudes are exhibited in similar ways in both dogs and people. In many ways, we learn things in the same fashion and that learning expresses itself in similar ways.

As an example, consider the pack behavior exhibited among canines that has been so visibly documented in recent years. Just how different is canine pack behavior and teenage gang behavior at its core? How different is the case of the adolescent dog trying to establish his identity, maybe even his dominance, in the pack and the adolescent human who demands to be treated as an adult and who begins to disrupt his own pack in a bid for a new identity? To take another tack, what is the appreciable difference between the older adult dog who has grown accustomed to routines and environment as stable things suddenly uprooted from them and the aging person who suddenly finds herself in a nursing home? Aren't both bewildered by new routines and angry about the lack of respect for the older, more comfortable ones that have been forcibly put aside without their consent? You bet they are. In the end, there may be more similarities between canine and human behavior, and ways to deal with them in your own pack at home than you might think.

This is a potentially unsettling idea. Someone is telling you that raising your children and raising your dog might really be much the same thing. If it is disturbing, that's understandable. After all, it's a scary thing to think that some of the behaviors you disapprove of in your dog might be the same kinds of behaviors your children could learn. Even worse, what if you're actually teaching these undesirable behaviors to one or the other, or both? Could such a thing actually happen? It could.

As we'll see, the learning process for dogs is as much a learning process for the dog's owners as it is anything else. Dog owners must discover how their dogs learn things so they can teach the manners they want their dogs to know. Interestingly, parents can, in some instances, see how to teach their children but can't see the same educational needs for their dogs.

For example, during training sessions in which owners are having difficulty understanding how their dogs are learning things from them, and if they also have children, we'll ask if their dogs know how to sit?

They reply, "Yes, he loves to sit."

If we've already seen a bit of this sit-loving dog, we'll ask: "If you ask your dog to sit, he'll sit, right?"

"Oh, yes," they say.

"Well, suppose there's a distraction. What do you do?"

"Well, I make him sit!"

"How do you do that? Do you push his butt down?"

"Yes."

"If you wanted him to lie down, would he lie down?"

"Well...uh, sometimes."

"But, if you really wanted him to lie down, you'd make him, right?"

"Oh, definitely. I'll make him lie down!"

"You'd, like, push him down? Make sure he laid down?"

"Right. That's what I'd do."

While we're chatting with them, we watch them interact with their dog. Sure enough, they'll give the sit command and then, when the dog doesn't do it, they'll push him down, making him sit, presumably to show us they're on top of their training. After a few minutes of this, one of us asks: "Well, let me ask you a question. If you have a child and you send him to clean his bedroom and he doesn't do it, would you go and clean it for him?"

"Well, no. No, of course not. Not on your life!"

"So, if you cleaned his room for him, you'd maybe be saying, 'That's okay, Honey, you don't have to do it; it's too hard for you to learn, so I'll do it for you. Right?"

Then one of us will put a hand out like we're pushing on the dog's rear-end and say: "That's okay, Honey. You don't have to sit yourself down. It's too hard for you to learn, so I'll do it for you."

You know what? That dog will never learn to do a sit on his own. Never, not *if* they always do it for him.

It's amazing what we seem to understand about raising kids, but don't equate with what we're teaching our other charges at home. This lack of understanding can be reversed. We may understand quite well that our four-legged kids can't possibly understand a concept like, "No, you must learn to act responsibly because it is personally and socially important to do so," and yet we expect such weighty matters to be understood and adopted by our young children, merely because we have commanded it.

In the end, if you've got dogs or children or both, you should start realizing what you're teaching them—or not teaching them. Maybe you can learn what you're doing with the one, by gaining some insight into what you're doing with the other. "Parenting," whether it's directed at your children or your dogs, is an important thing. Being a good parent, for both your dogs and your kids, is what this book is all about.

With children, the importance of good parenting is obvious to most folks. But, with dogs, some people might question: "Why bother? And why parenting, anyway? Can't I just get my dog trained by somebody if I don't like the way he's acting?" Answering this last question may help answer the first two questions.

For one thing, yes, you can get someone to train your dog for you, but is it that easy? Are there no magical instructions that can be imparted to your dog that, once learned, will allow you to make him do whatever you want him to do? Sorry, but it just doesn't work that way. You've got to be part of the process yourself or else no amount of training will do you the least bit of good. Occasionally, people come to our Academy of Canine Behavior intent on just dropping off their dogs for a month to be trained. They assume that when they pick up their dogs they'll be able to whisk them away home and all their dog troubles will be solved. We had one fellow do this just recently. He came by with his dog and said: "I hear that you guys do good work with dogs. I want to use your board-and-train program for my dog. I'll just drop him off and my housekeeper will pick him up in a month."

We had to explain that our board and train did not work quite like that. We suggested scheduling a time for him to come in for some training at the end of the second, third and fourth weeks.

"Sorry," he said, "but I'm going to be out of the country for a month."

"Well, that's fine, but when you get back you'll need to spend a visit with us, and then another visit, and then on the last visit you'll be able to take your dog home. After all, we've got a lot to teach you."

Regardless of the quality of professional training, you've got to be part of your dog's education. Without that, you'll never understand him and he'll never understand you.

Again, why bother to be involved? Why bother to be a parent? It's about responsibility to your kids— both the two- and four-legged ones. If your child wasn't behaving quite the way you'd like him to, or you moved to a new setting where it was inconvenient to have a child, would you get rid of him? Of course not. Yet, amazingly, that's just what some of you are prepared to do with your dogs.

You only have to visit one animal shelter to know that many people treat their dogs like Dixie cups—once they're done with them, they just throw them away. They might assume they're doing the right thing by taking their dog to a shelter. They figure: "It's just not working out. I can't keep him out of the azaleas and he's bitten the neighbor twice! Maybe someone else will have better luck with him. He'll get a good home and be much happier." Sadly, with 62 million cats and 53 million dogs out there, he'll stand a better chance of winning the lottery than he will just making it out of that shelter alive: There aren't enough homes for them all. In the United States, we *put to sleep*—just plain kill—between 10 and 20 million pets a year. Why? Because people don't want to bother with handling behavioral problems that ultimately spell the doom of millions of healthy, loving cats and dogs. It's time we started to bother.

This book isn't just about how to parent your dog. Because dogs and kids learn from us in similar ways, acquiring some insight into how to parent the one might help us when we're parenting the other. If you're not overly worried about what's happening to all those *throw-away* pets, maybe you should think about the possibility of raising a *throw-away* person. The behavioral problems that are costing the lives of all those cats and dogs just might be the very ones that you're unconsciously teaching your children right now. Understanding the source of the behavior problems in your dog, and how to deal with those problems, might just help you prevent or correct similar behavior problems in your kids.

Chapter 1
Pack Theory

If you're interested in talking to your kids—actually having them listen and understand what you're saying to them—you need to know how they think. Kids aren't miniature adults, even though some people try to treat them as if they were. Kids think differently from the way adults do. They think differently from adults because their lives are different. Dogs think differently from the way you do, too. And, in many ways their lives are very different from your own. However, in some important ways they see things around them in ways quite similar to how you see certain things. The trick is knowing what these things are. If you expect to communicate effectively with your dogs, you need to know how they understand the world around them and what they consider their place in it to be.

The vast majority of canine perception and learning is based on what is called pack behavior, and it's vital that you have some understanding of this if you are to parent your dogs successfully. Even though it's very important that you understand what pack behavior is all about, it's too complex to try to explain it all. Besides, you can get highly detailed information on the subject elsewhere, and for now it's only necessary that you have an understanding of some of the basic mechanisms that underlie and help structure pack behavior in general.

Canines are highly social animals. Dogs socialize with humans to a remarkable extent, but this socializing isn't just with humans, it's with each other as well. Canines live in family or extended-family groups. In the wild, this is true of wolves, jackals, dingoes and many other canines. Domesticated dogs also arrange themselves in social organizations or packs. These groups are tightly knit. They can be made up of several generations of individuals, living and working together as a unit. Packs are successful because of the cooperative nature of the members in the pack, in which each shares the load of the collective welfare of the whole pack.

People are also social animals. Up until quite recently in our own culture, family members stayed together as a unit, sometimes a very large one, possibly made up of several generations of family members. This is still the case in many cultures today. It has been only in the last few decades that it has become common for children, when they grow up and leave the family, to move any appreciable distance from the family's home. And, again, it has been only in the last few decades that it has become somewhat uncommon for the young married couple to live with one set of parents for a while, until they could get their feet on the ground and move into a home of their own. And, in Western culture since the earliest times, women joined the men's family upon marriage. This often included joining his extended family as well, with grandparents, parents, aunts, uncles and children all living under the same roof. Like canines, we are well accustomed to organizing ourselves into pack-like family groups.

As with human packs, among canines new packs may be established by the younger members of an already-existing pack, but it doesn't matter if it's a long-established pack or not, each one has a pair of recognized leaders, male and female. If you watch nature shows on television, chances are that sooner or later you'll see one about pack behavior in canines. If you have, you've likely heard the male and female leaders of the pack referred to as the *Alpha Male* and the *Alpha Female*.

While it is perfectly accurate to designate the male and female leaders of a pack as *alphas*, this may mislead you into thinking that dogs simply run down the Greek alphabet in clear lines of descending authority. This isn't the case. In the canine world, there is no linear thinking of this kind. Just because you are number three in the pack doesn't mean that you necessarily have authority over numbers four, five and six.

As a partial comparison, consider the members of your own pack at home. Daughter number one, a six-year old, doesn't necessarily have any authority or privileges over her two-year-old brother or her baby sister. And yet, neither are they strictly equals in the pack. In addition, while daughter number one may be called upon later to take on the responsibility of looking after her younger siblings, and thus be given some authority over them on a temporary basis, as she matures into adulthood, such authority, if it was ever really there, dissipates. For a time, relative age created a dynamic in the pack that compelled its members to adopt certain roles and responsibilities, but to say that daughter number one is dominant over the other two children would be inaccurate.

Among canines, the reality is that there are numerous pockets within the larger pack structure from which respect is drawn, and to which respect is in turn given. Here, age matters in terms of relative authority, just as it does to a certain degree among people; and, like people, these age differences really only affect levels of authority between the larger categories of youngsters, adolescents and adults. Among each category, other dynamics will determine authority, and again, the pecking order is not clearly laid out in a linear fashion. Say you have six puppies. The most dominant puppy will assert himself as *alpha* and have authority over puppies number two through six. Number two will be subservient to number one, but will have authority over numbers three, four, five and six. It might seem that this arrangement would simply continue on down the line, with puppy number six being submissive to everyone else, but it doesn't necessarily work out that way. For example, puppy number four may be dominant over puppies five and six, but number six may actually be dominant over puppy number three.

Individual dynamics of various types will determine this pecking order, just as individual dynamics among human groups create a complex web of individual strengths and weaknesses based on given needs and situations. Bob may be the strongest of the six buddies out camping together, but Bob can't swim a stroke. When it comes to crossing the river, it's one of the other guys out in front, pulling Bob along behind. The pecking order just changed, if only for a while. Within the pack, the male and female leaders will exert authority over different concerns and over other pack members of each one's respective gender. As a result, separate male and female hierarchies exist within the pack.

Among canines, and among many other species as well, nature intended for the male to be dominant. With both a male and a female hierarchy in the pack, the female has her set of rules and lines of authority, and the male has his, so who's doing what? Generally speaking, the *alpha* male tends to oversee the welfare and survival of the pack as a unit. He leads the hunt, protects the pack from invaders and maintains order among pack members. However, the *alpha* female is also in charge of the pack's welfare, but she takes care of concerns quite different from those that are the responsibility of the *alpha* male. The *alpha* female is responsible for breeding, and thus for the continuance of the pack in a very literal sense. She does not allow other females in the pack to have litters without her consent. She is in charge of establishing safe den sites, delegating puppy care-giving responsibilities to other pack members—when she's not doing it herself—and doing those things that among humans might be considered domestic chores.

The obvious human analogy to this division of labor is our traditional family lifestyle. The husband works and pays the bills, and the wife runs the household. In some cultures, the wife is given the only keys to the household upon marriage, signifying her supremacy in establishing and maintaining domestic affairs. The husband doesn't try to tell her what supplies to buy or how to bake bread, and the wife doesn't tell him how to run his business or earn an income. There has been a major shift in social and family dynamics in recent decades. Both women's and men's roles have changed. Both bake the bread these days and both run the businesses. However, dogs haven't experienced the same shift, and traditional family roles are still in effect for them. As a result, things that occur in the pack that might upset a female and make her very angry, a male might not even notice, or vice-versa. However, for reasons best known to Mother Nature, when pack concerns overlap both male and female responsibilities and are not clearly divided along gender-lines, the *alpha* male is the one who is ultimately in charge.

In the end, then, the social structure of the pack is determined by a variety of factors: gender, age and *alpha* leadership, the most important of which is the order established by the *alphas*. And, again, each has his or her own role and areas of authority to establish and maintain. For example, the *alpha* male will usually not discipline puppies. He may growl at them a bit or grudgingly get up to move out of the way if they're being too much of a nuisance to him, but a good male dog will not concern himself over their discipline. The female takes care of that; it falls under her authority to do so.

After the pups come to a certain age, however, he'll start to discipline them. He'll begin to discipline the adolescents. Among people, the analogy for this kind of shift in disciplinary roles is found in the old farming family. Back on the farm in days gone by, when the kids were still young they stayed inside and did household chores under mom's guidance. As soon as the kids, particularly the boys, were thought to be old enough, they began to do outside chores in the fields with dad. When that happened, they came under his authority. This is how it breaks down with dogs, too. With the pups, the female is quick to discipline them while the male just ignores them. As soon as they start becoming adolescents, however, you'll see the male start thumping them if he feels they have transgressed his authority, and the female gradually reduces disciplining them. Even so, by that time the female has established her rule over them as well.

The structure and mechanisms that hold the pack together don't change, but individuals and their roles in the pack do. Even as a puppy's role in the pack changes as it matures, so, too, do the pack roles among adults sometimes change. This most often occurs in a challenge for leadership. Challenges to the *alpha* leadership can occur for a variety of reasons. Sometimes it is simply a result of natural processes: The current leader is getting older and more feeble and is seen as no longer capable of leading the pack successfully. Or, a challenge may arise if the *alpha* is injured or ill. In still other instances, pack members may question the *alpha's* right to lead if he is seen as inconsistent or has made bad choices that affect the welfare of the pack, like leading them into a series of unsuccessful hunts. A high-ranking dog might actively challenge the *alpha* out of an innate desire to be top dog himself. Just as often, other kinds of changes—a new location, addition of new pack members, splitting of the pack and so on—can bring a shift in any or all of the individuals' place in the dominance pecking order. Dogs desire—no, actually *require*—structure in their lives and to know where they stand in the pack at all times, otherwise confusion and/or fear emerges. In short, dogs become uncomfortable, sometimes in alarming ways for our pack at home, if they are left unsure of their role in the pack. Changes in the pack, even something as simple as moving to a new location, may create a challenge to *alpha* leadership because other pack members wish to reaffirm their positions. We'll talk much more about this later on.

Being the leader of the pack requires that the leader constantly communicate his or her authority over other pack members. With people, at least with those people who are unaccustomed to leadership, this kind of behavior might be regarded as someone being a bit too uppity. However, among pack members it is both necessary and desirable for the smooth operation of a unit of many individuals. Just ask a military officer how important it is to communicate authority to those of lower rank. Without that authority in place, dissension and indecision cripple the unit's ability to accomplish its goals. Demonstrating leadership is a form of instruction for the *alphas*. It allows them to instruct others in how things can be successfully accomplished, and it instills confidence in the other pack members that someone competent is in charge of their collective welfare. And, the demonstration of this authority by the *alphas* is also a way of preventing potential behavioral transgressions that might endanger the smoothly running nature of the pack, or of correcting those transgressions that do occur.

One way pack leaders demonstrate authority over other pack members is by going first. **Leaders always go first.** Whether it's leading the hunt, eating the kill, moving in a particular direction, initiating play, greeting others or establishing territory, leaders go first. The knowledge that leaders go first is also understood quite well by most people, even if they haven't actually been taught such things in a direct fashion. Imagine a group of employees walking down a corridor with their boss. As they come to the site of the big meeting, who goes through the door first? The boss, of course. Imagine everyone else barging in ahead. Do you call the boss into your office, or does he call you into his? You know the answer to that one, too.

In a pack environment, the dominant male has the best spot to lay in the denning area. It is usually the ledge in the sun, the driest and the warmest spot—in every way it's the best. The other members of the pack will radiate out from that spot, just as ministers or cabinet members radiate out in descending order of rank and importance from their leader (who occupies the central position at the negotiating table directly across from his or her foreign counterpart). **Leaders occupy the highest ground**, even as kings and queens sit on a raised dais while conducting affairs of state. Height equals might, and the leader demonstrates authority by always taking the most prominent position.

Leaders initiate everything, even those things that you might consider frivolous and insignificant, such as play and greetings. But, again, it seems as if you instinctively understand that sort of behavior among yourselves. When the *alpha* greets others, there is a noticeable submission response from pack members. Crouching or rolling on their backs to expose their vitals demonstrate obvious recognition of one who has the power to do his will with them. The leader will lay his muzzle atop the one being greeted, again showing that height equals might. Compare this action with patting someone on the head. It's usually all right to do so with a small child, but if you did it to a friend or peer it would be taken as an insult. They would think you were being condescending to them. We pat those we consider to be somehow in our care and under our authority, not peers and certainly not our superiors. The same is true among canines.

Similarly, handshakes as greetings follow rules of pack leadership. Does the employee squeeze the boss's hand as hard as possible to demonstrate relative strength, or does the employee hold back enough to show respect? And how about play? Again, leaders initiate even this, or accept overtures by other pack members to play as it suits their whim. A *beta* or even an *omega* may come to the *alpha* to request play, but it is always at his discretion if play will actually take place. And, if the *alpha* initiates play through posturing, such as the play bow or through vocalizations, chances are that the other pack members will follow his lead and begin to play. A break has been called for. Again, this is also true with people. Does the employee take a break whenever he feels like it, or does the boss establish when such breaks will be taken? You know the answer to that one, too. Leaders go first and they make all the rules.

Leaders lead. It's as simple as that. However, it's the most important thing that goes on in the pack. Pack behavior is the means by which dogs come to learn their roles in life. It is a constant process of learning one's place, and it is constantly reinforced for them by pack leaders and other members of the pack. This kind of instruction is vital to a dog's well-being. It instills a sense of comfort and confidence in them that they are where they should be and that a competent leader is looking out for them. When you become the leaders in your pack at home, it is your responsibility to lead well and to set up the rules and abide by them in a consistent fashion so that other members of the pack can be comfortable in their roles and confident in your ability to lead them. In short, setting yourself up at home as pack leader for your dog is the best thing you can do. It's best for both your dog's peace of mind, because he will understand you and feel good about his relationship with you as a result, and your own peace of mind because you will have a happy, cooperative pack member who is easy to live with. In fact, being pack leader and setting up the structures your dog will live by are the best ways to say you care to your dog. The same is true with kids. Allowing an unstructured life, with no rules and a do-whatever-you-want attitude toward your kids translates: "I don't care enough about you to bother putting myself out to guide your upbringing." We'll talk a lot more about this structuring of our kids' lives, both the two- and four-legged kind, later in the book. We'll also come to see just how important it is for you to become the *alpha* in your pack—a good, caring, consistent, authoritative *alpha*.

Chapter 2
Developmental Timelines

While having some sense of how pack behavior works is very useful, you should also know something about how your dogs mature physically and mentally so you will understand how things are influencing them at any given moment in their development. This is important because it will help you understand what kinds of things you should and shouldn't be doing with them at various points in their lives. This is vital to your ability to be good parents to them. This is true with your other kids at home, too. You need to know what your dogs and kids are thinking about their world as they grow up, and also what things are having an impact on their lives at various stages in their development.

Earliest Stages: Birth to Seven Weeks

When a puppy is born, he is simply an organism that instinctively seeks warmth and nourishment. A newborn puppy is so helpless that even elimination is left entirely to his mother, who licks the puppy's abdomen to stimulate urination and bowel movements. It's important to remember just how helpless these little creatures are. You all know just how helpless a human baby is, but for some reason you tend to think that other animals are different because they mature so quickly. You need to keep in mind that puppies require lots of attention, just like human babies.

At three weeks of age, the puppy's nervous system comes "online." At 21 days, this magical event takes place for all canines. Before this, there have been little scattered pockets of information coming and going in the puppy's brain, but only minimal communication between them. On the 21st day, the nervous system matures to the point of linking up all the existing systems. It can be likened to the driving of the golden spike that symbolized the completion of the first transcontinental railroad. At this point, the puppy is beginning to climb out of the whelping box and things are starting to happen *fast*.

Between 21 and 35 days, the puppy matures quickly, both physically and mentally. During this time the puppy spends most of his time mastering physical coordination. Now that his nervous system is connected, he's trying to figure out how to use it. Before the driving of the golden spike, the puppy may have wanted to walk across the whelping box, but would get only halfway there, fall over and forget where he was going. Not any more. Now he picks himself up and keeps going until he gets where he wants to go.

During this stage, interaction with littermates is increasing rapidly as the puppies master the coordination to play. They are also beginning to learn important information about themselves and those around them from both their mother and their littermates. It is never a good idea to remove the puppy from his environment at this time because important information needed by the puppy will be lost if he is separated from the source of that information. Vital information that should be learned would then become the responsibility of the human parent. Are you willing to do that? Do you know what he's supposed to be learning right now, and could you teach it to him? Best to leave this part of the puppy's education to the experts—his mother and littermates.

During the developmental period from about five to seven or eight weeks, the puppy is learning all kinds of things about himself: where he stands in the pack among the other puppies, how to get along with others, and also how strong he is. If removed from the litter now, you may face some real behavioral challenges down the road.

During this time, the puppy is focused on playing games with his littermates. Now that they are all becoming more physically coordinated, they can play in earnest. Now the games are becoming more serious. When they play tug-of-war, it really does matter who wins. If one puppy has something and runs with it, all the other puppies will try to get it from him: possession of anything is a mark of dominance, both for now and in the future. They start playing king of the hill: one puppy will get up on something, daring the others to come up after him. Height is might, and a physical prominence may pan out to be a higher ranking in the pecking order later on. Domination games of all kinds emerge and evolve during this period, and the outcome of these games help establish a dog's sense of his role in the pack structure. In addition, it's worth noting that it's not always the biggest or the strongest puppy who dominates. Many times it's just the cleverest who prevails.

Another very important lesson the puppy learns during this stage is how strong he is and how painful his bite can be. He learns to use an inhibited bite. If he bites down too hard on the other puppies, they won't play with him. They scream and yelp, "Go away and leave me alone. You hurt me!" They run to their mother, who tells the rowdy one, "Gruff (Enough)!" This is how a puppy learns that even though he can grab hold and shake an object, he shouldn't bite down too hard with those needle-sharp little teeth. If you get a puppy of five weeks or even younger, you'd better be prepared to face a dog who bites and learn how to correct this behavior early on. Otherwise, you're headed for disaster and your dog is headed for an untimely end. In addition, you will need to take on much of the puppy's socialization, which he would have gotten from following his mother around and interacting with littermates. Socialization is how puppies get to know new things and how to get along with others at a very young age. Even as a little kid needs to become socially mature so his behavior is acceptable, so, too, does a puppy need to be socialized. Without this socialization, problems will occur as the puppy gets older.

Middle Stages: Eight to Sixteen Weeks

The developmental period from eight to eleven weeks is called the Fear Imprint Stage. It is the time in a puppy's life when he can encounter something—almost anything—that frightens him, and remain frightened by that thing for the rest of his life. It is our belief that this stage in domestic canines finds its parallel in wild canines during the period when they first start to leave the den and explore their nearby surroundings. As they start exploring, it's necessary for those wild canines to develop fears for certain things, or they're not going to survive very long: "My, what an interesting creature to play with, it's got a rattle on one end! And what's that large shape flying overhead and hurtling toward me? I wonder if it wants to play?" While fearlessness makes for great heroes in the movies, in the wild it might mean a shortened life. Nature intended for us to learn how to fear certain things as a way of helping us survive. Just as pain tells us that we're injured, fear tells us how to avoid injury.

Fear imprint on a puppy can manifest itself in several different ways. If you're walking down the street with your puppy and a big, black dog comes along, grabs your puppy and shakes him, you can bet that this incident is going to have some sort of lasting impact on the little guy. The question, though, is just what kind of fear might he develop as a result of such an experience? Will he develop a fear of big, black dogs? Will he develop a fear of big dogs, or maybe just black dogs? Maybe he'll develop a fear of walking down the street, or maybe just that one street. The problem is that you can't just bend down and ask him what he's afraid of as a result of his encounter with the big, black dog. It's terribly frustrating to have no way of influencing the impact of that event on your puppy's mind. You might be able to control the information his brain receives, but you have no control at all over how he processes that information.

Imagine a puppy chasing a bird into a holly bush. He dives into the bush and gets painfully stuck. Afterwards, he pulls himself free. At this point, he may be thinking several different things: a) I'm never going to chase birds again; b) I'm never going to go into a holly bush again; or c) bushes and birds are bad for you. You simply cannot know which thought occurred to him at the moment he got out of that holly bush. However, you may very well see the result of this encounter come to the surface later on when you're training him. As a result, since you cannot read his mind even though you may have witnessed the event yourself, no single training technique can be applied to all dogs to help them overcome their fears or change the behavior that results from these fears.

We have an Irish Water Spaniel named *Flirt,* who as a puppy was very outgoing. When she was nine weeks old, we put her outside in an exercise pen. A big dog came out of a nearby car and headed toward her. Flirt, always friendly, bounced up against the wire panel of the pen to greet the newcomer, tail wagging like mad: "Hi, how are you?" That big dog hit the exercise pen so hard that it knocked her clear across it. To this day, and Flirt is almost 10 years old, she still cringes and tucks her tail between her legs if any large dog comes running toward her. The impact of this event on Flirt has never diminished, even with two professional trainers in the house to help. The Fear Imprint Stage is a very impressionable point in a puppy's life, and you need to take real care in what you're doing with your dog during this time, or you may accidentally create unnecessary fears that surface later on and interfere with training.

You can't think of everything and you can't insulate your puppy from all the things in the world that might potentially cause him to develop a specific fear of something. For example, take the case of a puppy who is snooping around a broom and accidentally knocks it over. It falls on him and startles him. The puppy may be afraid of brooms forever after. Later on, if we're not familiar with what happened, we might see the fear surface and think: "Somebody has been beating this poor dog with a broom!" You can't insulate your puppy from everything, and chances are that he will not pass through this stage without being afraid of *something*.

You really don't want to isolate your puppy during this time. The Fear Imprint Stage is a time of rapid learning for your puppy, and so he needs to be experiencing all he can as part of his socialization. Even so, this is not the time to introduce him to a potentially fearful situation, such as bringing him into a place where there are children acting wildly. On the other hand, a calmer, more controlled introduction to kids at this point can be a very good thing, again, helping your puppy to get properly socialized to being around kids. Just use common sense with him during this time. Take him out to the pond and let him play in the water if he wants, but don't toss him in the water or splash him, thinking that you're helping him overcome his hesitation towards the pond—you're doing just the opposite. As pack leader, your puppy is counting on you not to place him in a potentially dangerous situation. You certainly don't want him to become fearful of you. Respectful, yes, but not fearful.

By about the 11th week, your puppy is ready for yet another big change. He's made it through the Fear Imprint Stage, but there's more to come. Until now, when you've been taking him for walks he's been staying right with you. When you've called him, he couldn't wait to come rushing back to his leader. Now, however, he doesn't seem to want to do that as much. How come? By about the 11th or 12th week, independence strikes. Look out! Your puppy is starting to cut the apron strings. The little sweetie who used to follow wherever you went and come whenever you called is suddenly turning into a completely different dog. It's really not that he won't come to you, it's just that he's got to see this other thing first, and just get in one more sniff of this. At this stage, your puppy's agenda is changing rapidly, and his behavior is, too.

Many times when we're doing a one-hour lesson called a Puppy Private with clients at the Academy, we'll describe this developmental stage to them and the clients will quickly recognize that that's what's been going on with their dogs. Often, this is exactly the reason they brought their dogs in to us. All of a sudden their cute little puppies started ignoring them, and the parents had no idea what to do about it.

From about 11 to 16 weeks, your puppy is in his final developmental stage as a puppy. At 16 weeks learning changes from long term to short term, so by the end of his 16th week, his personality is unlikely to go through any more radical changes. Even though he may still look puppyish to you, he's not a puppy any more, and it's time to stop treating him like one. Up to this point, you've been molding him and making impressions on him about who you are and what his relationship is to you. Now he is fast approaching full adulthood, and he is ready for training in earnest.

Latter Stages: Approaching Adulthood and Old Age

From about four to six months of age, a dog's life is comparable to that of an elementary school-age child: both youngsters are still doing a lot of developing and are trying hard to master a range of skills. Nature has provided them with seemingly inexhaustible amounts of energy for this stage in their lives, because they have so much to learn in a relatively short amount of time. By the end of this time, your dog's physical horizons will have expanded and he will begin to test your authority regularly to make sure if you are really in charge after all, or to see if his own role in the pack is changing now that he is coming into his full adulthood. It is vital at this point, and really throughout the remainder of his life, that you remain consistent with him, reinforcing good behavior and reminding him constantly of the rules.

At this point, it's also worth noting that different breeds develop at different rates. The last time all breeds of dogs are truly developmentally equal in their lives is the day of the driving of the golden spike on their 21st day. After that, differences in development are determined to some degree by both gender and breed. Just like people, female dogs tend to mature more quickly than male dogs. In addition, some breeds seem to develop more quickly than others. In general, smaller breeds have a faster maturation rate than do the larger breeds. On average, you can expect a Cocker Spaniel or a Miniature Poodle to mature more quickly than a Mastiff or a Great Dane. As a rule, however, by nine months your dogs are full-blown teenagers, no matter what breed you have.

Another developmental change to watch for as your dog matures is the onset of puberty. Many canines will go through a second fearful stage at this time. If you've ever heard anyone refer to the "teenage weirds," this is the time they meant. Maybe this second fearful stage, coming as it does at the onset of puberty, is nature's way of helping preserve the species. Both canine and human teenagers tend to believe they are 10-feet tall and bulletproof. This is a dangerous attitude to maintain for very long. Because it is dangerous, nature imparts a sense of vulnerability at this point to keep those teenagers from sticking their necks out too far.

Don't worry, you'll know when your dog is heading into this stage. You'll come home and find your dog cringing and barking like mad at the sack of groceries you just left on the kitchen floor. You'll have an acquaintance drop by for a visit and your dog will assume he's an ax-murderer. You'll see someone pass your dog on the sidewalk with a baby stroller, and he'll react as if it were filled with sea monsters. You'll see your dog act as if the paperboy was suddenly throwing things at *him*, and not the front porch. You'll know. For those who enter their dogs in dog shows, this can be a particularly frustrating time. Imagine your promising, young show dog, who only weeks before was acting as if everyone was his best buddy, won't let a ring judge get within 20 feet of him, let alone examine him.

Matters can get pretty tricky during this time. This is also the time when a dog may be trying out his role as a watchdog. If not taken in hand and guided through this stage, a dog may become a fearful watchdog instead of a confident one. A fearful dog is like a fearful person in that he usually stops thinking when confronted by a strange situation. Instead, he just reacts, often with tragic results. Imagine a young soldier with a loaded gun who has been through only the most rudimentary training so far. Put him in a volatile situation, such as a riot in which he is confronted by an apparently hostile crowd of people. Take away his commander. Would you want to be in that crowd, knowing that he has a loaded gun? Now give him back his commander—someone who is confident and a seasoned veteran. The commander's experience gives him the ability to read the crowd and to assess the potential threat and know how to deal with it. He is able to help the young soldier make the right decisions.

If a dog has a solid temperament, this stage will pass with no real lasting impact. However, anything less than a solid temperament in your dog makes it extremely important how you respond to his behavior while he's in this stage. One of the biggest mistakes people make at this time, and during the initial Fear Imprint Stage, is trying to talk the dog out of being afraid of something. Cooing at your dog when he's afraid as a way of trying to calm him, like you would with a frightened child, is actually reinforcing his fears. The same is true with petting or stroking him in a similar situation. Those are reward responses from you, the same kind you'd give when your dog did something right during training sessions. You're telling your dog that he did something right by being afraid when you comfort him. He assumes that you must like his behavior, because every time he starts acting weird you talk gently to him and pet him. If you do this, what starts out as a problem related to his development quickly evolves into a problem with his education.

Another mistake you may make when responding to a dog's weird behavior is to overreact to it. If you start yelling and jumping around,

Yikes! another monster...
I must be in my Fear Imprint Stage.

your dog will believe that you also have been upset by the triggering stimulus. He will believe that his own reaction is correct, because the pack leader is also acting weird, and pack leaders know what's what, right? You've seen this kind of response when two people with dogs meet. The dogs begin sizing up one another and eventually one of them feels that the other isn't being properly respectful to him or his space, and a scuffle breaks out. Unfortunately, the two owners may start yelling and screaming at the dogs. Both dogs then figure that their pack leaders are either exhorting them on to fuller efforts to maintain their dignity, or else are duking it out for reasons best left to pack leaders to understand. You unwittingly reinforce negative behavior by—to their way of thinking—joining in the scuffle.

The first thing you should do when your dog starts acting weird about something is to, firmly but calmly, let him know that you disapprove of that behavior. Often, just a simple, "No, knock it off," is all it takes. Once you've negated his behavior, then have him do a simple action, like a sit. Once he's done so, praise him by saying, "Good sit." Make sure you've got the word *sit* in there, or he may think you're praising him for the fear he likely still feels from his run-in with whatever it was that set him off in the first place. Don't force him to face up to the thing that frightened him. Allow him to just sit and observe while you approach the thing, person or animal confidently in a positive manner. Be the role model for the response you would like your dog to have. By occasional quiet and calm reinforcement of the sit with verbal praise, he's able to re-evaluate the situation calmly without you distracting him. Don't overreact with the praise, either. If you do, your dog might think that something out of the ordinary is going on. If you act like it's no big deal, chances are that your dog will, too.

We get more dogs at the Academy at nine months of age than any other age group except for puppies. It is the next most troublesome age for problem behavior. The parents have grown accustomed to their cute little puppy, and they would still like to treat him like one, but he's not a puppy any more. He is a teenager whose physical development is pushing buttons like mad all through his system. If your dog hasn't been spayed or neutered, you're going to have to learn how to deal with the onset of a blast of reproductive hormones. Mother Nature takes a long look at a Golden Retriever who is still intact and thinks:

> Hmmmm, a Golden Retriever has an estimated life span of about 13 years, and he's going to need some testosterone. Let's see, over that amount of time he's going to need about 20 thousand units of testosterone to see him through. WHAM! Here it is.

Spaying or neutering your dog will in no way stop his physical or mental development. Some people think that it puts your dog on hold as a pre-teen for the rest of his life. While spaying and neutering helps you get a hold on hormonally stimulated behavior problems, an altered dog will still become a teenager in other behavioral respects.

A nine-month-old dog has one foot in puppyhood and the other three firmly in adulthood. It's a tricky time for both him and you because it is such a transitional period, just as it is with your other teenagers at home. This is the time when many dogs end up in shelters, soon to be destroyed, because the behavioral problems that may emerge during this time can be unbearable for the dog's owners. This is really the making or breaking point with some dog owners. If you can survive your dog's teenage stage, by guiding him firmly through it, he might turn out to be the best dog you ever had. If you can't survive this phase, well, don't kid yourself about what's going to happen with your dog.

We get many teenage dogs in at the Academy, mostly because teenagers just aren't a whole heck of a lot of fun to live with when they're out of control. Many people who have given up on their dogs at this point try to fool themselves by thinking: We'll just take him to the shelter; they'll find a good home for him. No, the chances are they won't. There just aren't enough homes for them all. Even more whimsical is the old "we'll find a home for him in the country." Just how many country homes do you think there are? The fact is, if you can't buckle down and work through this stage, chances are your dog's going to end up on the wrong end of a syringe.

Fortunately, there are things you can do to make this stage better for both you and your dog. The first thing you can do is realize that you don't have a puppy anymore. People seem to have a hard time accepting this transition. We had a client come in with her nine-month-old Labrador. All through her conversation about her troubles with her dog, she kept referring to him as a puppy. We kept telling her: "No, you don't have a puppy anymore, you've got a teenager. That's different." At first, she was willing to agree, but her very next statement was about her puppy again. She could say teenager, but she just couldn't accept the fact. She was thinking in human terms—when you're nine months old, you're just a baby. Sadly, she had been treating her adult dog like a helpless baby and things were rapidly falling apart between her and her dog. She was unwilling to exert any type of control over her baby.

While this was unfortunate for a Labrador, it would likely be fatal for a Rottweiler. If you don't establish your leadership and control over your six-month-old, cute-as-a-button Rotty pup, you're likely headed for disaster. Personally, we're convinced that Rottweiler puppies are the cutest, sweetest little things that ever wriggled and wagged a tail, but if you've got a young Rottweiler you've got to get on top of him mentally, right away, because when he makes his transition into adulthood he will definitely become very pushy. This happens with Rottweilers all the time. People become afraid of their dogs because they are out of control teenagers. If your Rottweiler begins to dominate you, your life becomes extremely risky.

If you think that's risky, how about a hormonally out of control teenager in your house? He has no manners and no sense of anyone else's needs. He wants to be an adult, and sometimes even acts like one, but he also wants to be treated like a child sometimes. This is only natural. We all go through it. But a teenager with no manners? A teenager with no sense of self-disipline. That's a bad situation all the way around. On the other hand, it's something special when your teenager exhibits some manners and a certain degree of social maturity. The same is true with your dog, particularly your dog who needs your control over him. You need to learn how to establish that control early on in your dog's life.

The conclusion of the trip to adulthood arrives at about 24 months. It's been a fast trip, but a lot has happened. When you and your dog have managed to survive this transition to adulthood, you can expect a fairly stable life together, depending on what you've been teaching your dog along the way, until he is about five or six years of age. But, there are still two important developmental stages left. The next one is your dog's mid-life crisis.

All kinds of strange, undesirable behaviors crop up when your dog gets to be about six years old, and this is the second largest group of adult dogs we see at the Academy. Mid-life crisis in a dog often seems to coincide with some change that has occurred in the pack at home. Someone has left the house, or someone new has come into the house who wasn't there before. Your dog is highly sensitive to both emotional stress and structural changes in the pack. A dog's mid-life crisis is usually a reaction to instability, change and family dynamics. If the dynamics in the family remain stable, then usually your dog does too. But divorce, separation, childbirth, moving to a new home, someone going off to college, tension among family members can create trauma in your dog. Happily, behavior problems due to mid-life crisis are the easiest to resolve in most cases.

It's fascinating just how profoundly family dynamics can affect your dog. With dogs this age coming in to the Academy, one of the first things we ask owners is have there been any major events or changes for the family. Events that you might consider major a dog might simply ignore. However, the reverse is often true. Remember, troublesome behavior that surfaces in a dog at this age doesn't spring from something in your perception, but rather from what the dog perceives.

We are constantly amazed by this disparity in perception between dogs and people and what each one thinks of as a major event. We'll ask a client if there have been any changes recently. Almost without exception, they say no. Then, as we're talking, we'll discover that someone has just had cancer surgery or that someone has gone off to college. Many clients have difficulty seeing a connection between these things and their dog's behavior, or maybe they just didn't think that their dog would notice. Dogs notice. And, they don't like change. Packs are supposed to be stable, made comfortable by routine and everyone knowing their place. Change disrupts routine, and consequently disrupts the pack in your dog's eyes. We've even seen mature dogs react negatively to the simple act of the family getting a new car.

There we are, trying to figure out what has set off some strange behavior in a client's dog, and then we discover that the poor dog has lost his car—the car that he used to ride in to the grocery store and on trips to the park. All of a sudden his car isn't there any more. Instead, there's this new thing sitting in the driveway looking and smelling strange. It's not his car. He doesn't know what to think. To him, it's more than just the loss of his car, it's also the loss of a piece of his territory. Sometimes you have to delve deep, but there's usually a good reason for your dog's behavior. At least, it's a good reason to him.

Once we received a call from a woman who was having trouble with her older Golden Retriever. We were already familiar with this dog because she had brought him in for help getting him through his teenage transition. Until she called that day, we assumed that things had been going well between her and her dog. She affirmed that her dog had just recently taken up the practice of using the living room carpet as his personal toilet. The dog had never acted this way before, and the woman was quite upset about it. Eventually we asked her what had changed in her household. It was very quiet on the other end of the line. Finally, she said: "Well, my husband left me." Bingo. Sure enough, the dog's misbehavior started at the same time her husband left. Her dog was picking up on her stress and the intense dislike she was feeling towards her husband. Also, when dogs sense a change in the pack or in territory issues, it's normal for them to use urine as a way of feeling grounded to a place again. In the end, the woman felt as if she understood her dog a little better than before. We still needed to deal with the dog's behavior, because simply understanding its cause was no excuse for it to continue.

Dogs are much more sensitive to things going on in your pack at home than you probably realize. They pick up on all kinds of things, and during this time some of the things that are going on in your pack may actually cause negative behavior in them.

After your dog's mid-life crisis, you can expect a fairly stable life with him once again until he becomes a senior dog. Old age differs for dogs depending on the breed and what sort of life they've had. For most dogs, old age can be considered to be anywhere from 10 to 18 years of age, but some of the larger breeds, like Great Danes, have a considerably shorter life span than Jack Russell Terriers This new stage brings new problems for the senior dog, many of which we face ourselves. Adjustments must be made because of aging and health issues—hearing and vision impairment, arthritis, kidney and bladder problems, diabetes, poor teeth. All the ailments we dread in our own lives are also potential problems for the older dog.

Senior dogs feel more vulnerable. Many of the behavior problems we see with older dogs are the same seen in injured dogs. They have a sense that they can no longer compete from a physical standpoint; they are slower, sometimes in pain, and self-esteem is ebbing.

This stage in a dog's life requires understanding, consideration and respect. Your dog deserves to live out his life reaping the rewards of a lifetime of devotion, which is appropriate in the give-and-take of life.

A dog's physical and mental development is a fast-paced and complex process. It is fraught with danger and intrigue, but if handled properly it can be a joy to watch as your dog grows with you. These first two chapters have tried to give you some insight into what's going on in your dog's life and mind as he develops. It's important to have some understanding of how your dog perceives the world around him, how he goes about learning things, and how this perception and learning changes and develops as he grows and develops. With this information, you can understand better how to communicate effectively with your dogs. Being a parent is being an educator and, as you'll see, you have lots to teach your two- and four-legged kids. As you go along, you'll come to see how you can educate all your kids at home so that the pack can live in harmony.

PART II
COMMUNICATION & EDUCATION

Introduction

For most of you, it's a conscious choice to have kids. You plan for it, you count on it, and you work for it. Because you choose to have kids, you also choose to accept responsibilities when they come along— it's a package deal. Once you have kids, there's no turning back. You can't ship them back to the factory if you're not happy with the model or style. These are big-time responsibilities. You're not only legally liable and responsible for your kids, you're ethically responsible for their educations so they learn to be accountable and take responsibility for themselves someday. You also choose to have a dog, and you have real responsibilities toward him, too, maybe more than you counted on at first. But, like your kids, there's no turning back with your dogs, either. While it's true that sometimes people make the wrong choices in breeds of dogs find solutions through separation, if you get yourself a dog plan for signing on for a 13- to 20-year hitch. It's a big deal, make no mistake. If you get a dog with the understanding that you're going to have him as a part of your family for the rest of his life— and we hope that you do—you need to learn how to parent him if you ever hope to have a happy life together.

As a parent, one of your primary tasks is being a communicator to your kids. You try to communicate the right things: what's right and what's wrong; how to find peace of mind; what the rules are for living well; how to get along with others, and much more. You try to communicate to them a code of behavior that will serve as a foundation for the rest of their lives. In fact, you're communicating to them all the time, even when you don't realize it, and sometimes when you wish you weren't. This is also true with your dogs.

Because you are communicating to them constantly, it's important to communicate well, for at least two reasons. First, if you communicate poorly, understanding breaks down on both sides of the parent-child relationship and conflicts will result. If you don't accurately communicate your intentions and desires for your kids, behavior problems in your children will emerge and you'll be sending them the wrong messages. They'll either fail to learn what you want them to, or else they'll learn all the wrong things. You're actually capable of teaching them negative behaviors if you communicate poorly. Second, you want to communicate accurately and effectively with your kids because you want your pack at home to be harmonious and you want it to run well. You want a home in which everyone knows what's going on and in which everyone feels comfortable with both themselves and the other members of the pack. In order to avoid the one and achieve the other, you need to see what you're communicating to your dogs and your other kids, and also what you're sometimes not communicating to them. You need to learn how to be good communicators in order to be good parents.

Chapter 3
Becoming Alpha & Staying That Way

Most behavior problems in your dog, and many of them in your other kids, are the direct result of failing to establish respect for your authority, either from an inability, a lack of desire, or a lack of clear education on how to do so.

Nothing is more important to being a good parent than being the leader of the pack. You must actually want to establish respect for your authority among your kids, and you must take on the responsibility of being the authority figure in the pack. If you don't accept this responsibility—and it's a big one—you can count on being ignored. When that happens, anything and everything that you want from your kids, and everything that you know is in their best interests, will be ignored. The same is true with your dog. Do you really think your dog is going to obey you out of some sense of his own enlightened self-interest? Not a chance.

Do you really think your kids are going to eat those beets instead of potato chips because they realize the need for iron and Vitamins A and C in their diets? No way. On the contrary, obedience in both your dogs and your kids will only happen if they are convinced that you are in charge. Why should your kids do otherwise? Why should your dog do otherwise? Potato chips are fun, and so is digging that monstrous hole in the garden and chasing the neighbor's kid. Your kids are not going to look out for their own best interests. They can't. They don't even know what *is* in their own best interests. Neither does your dog. And if you're not the authority figure, if you're not really the leader of the pack, why should they bother listening to you? If you want to be listened to and obeyed, you need the pack to respect your authority. You need to become the *alpha*.

Having said that, it's probably a good idea at this point to allay some potential fears about what's going on when you establish respect for your authority. As you'll see, being respected and establishing your authority aren't matters of physical punishment or even domination. They are matters of communicating effectively.

As you saw in Chapter 1, dogs see others around them as pack members. This is how canines instinctively understand their world and their relationship with others. Dogs learn their roles in the pack—whether in the wild or in your home—from this instinctive understanding of how packs should be organized, and by being instructed as to what their particular place is in the pack. It's an interactive instruction for them: both the individual dog and the other pack members interact in a way to establish their roles and have their roles established for them.

To be comfortable and happy, a dog needs to know where he stands in the pack. To know this, he needs to know who's boss. A dog's attitude toward being introduced to a new pack, like you and your other family members, is essentially a take-me-to-your-leader approach. Dogs require pack leaders to understand their roles. Becoming that leader is the best thing you can do for your dog. Remember, he's going to be a lot more comfortable and a lot happier knowing that he can rest easy because the good ol' pack leader has everything under control. Your dog wants a leader around because pack leaders look after the pack and its welfare; having a leader looking out for you is a good feeling.

The dog's attitude of "who's in charge around here, anyway" is a natural one. He wants to know who's in charge because that will help tell him what his role is supposed to be and who to turn to in times of need. If a dog can't find an easily recognizable pack leader, a dominant dog may begin to assume: "Well, it looks like *I'm* in charge around here. Not bad, not bad at all." Even a less dominant dog might begin to take charge of the pack if he can't recognize a pack leader, less from a desire to be top dog himself than from a sense of need: packs require leadership if they're going to be successful, and *somebody's* got to take charge. If this happens, your dog is certainly not going to listen to the so-called commands of one of his underlings—namely you. The same is going to be true of your other charges at home. Without communicating to them that you're the leader and that they need to respect your authority as the leader, they have no one to answer to but themselves, and they're certainly not going to pay much attention to you. Why should they?

A client came to this realization herself while talking about her problems with her new dog: "I've never had problems with any of my other dogs before. I've raised all my kids and I..." All of a sudden she realized the answer: "I know why this dog doesn't mind me! My kids aren't around anymore. Every other dog I've ever had has watched me parent my kids and knew that I was the one in control. This dog has never seen me with my kids, so he doesn't understand who's in charge." She knew right then that she had to start communicating her leadership again.

Because you learn from your mistakes, it's a good idea to understand some of the ways you communicate disrespect for your leadership, and some of the consequences of doing so. One common mistake people make is employing empty threats. This is a sure-fire way of setting yourself up for failure with both your kids and your dog. If for any reason you make a threat, you'd darn well better be able and willing to carry it out. If you're not, then it's an empty threat and carries no weight or authority. Pretty soon, everyone knows it, too. Once you've taught your youngster that you don't really mean what you say, there's no reason why he should ever bother to pay attention to you. The person who makes a threat that is beyond doing, obviously doesn't have to carry out the threat. There's no obligation to, because it can't be done. How convenient: Now you don't have to take charge at all. Your kids feel free to do anything they want because they know that not only do you not mean what you say, but you don't want to do anything about their behavior in the first place.

It is difficult trying to work with people who don't want to take charge. Sometimes it's obvious that they don't want to take charge of their children, so it's like talking to a brick wall to get them to understand that they have to take charge of their dog. Many clients come in with incorrigible children. Even though they've come to us to fix their dogs, they never notice that the same problems they're having with their dogs are evident in their kids, too.

One client came in with her three-year old to discuss some problems she was having with her dog. It was nearing the Christmas holidays and we were in the process of moving. As a result, the only place we could put up our personal Christmas tree was in the lobby of the Academy. When the mother came in with her child, it became obvious that we were going to need to warn him away from the Christmas tree. He was all over the place and his mother couldn't—or wouldn't—control him. We had some rather valuable ornaments on the tree and didn't want the little guy to break them. We told him to leave the tree alone, but he just walked right over to it and reached out for the ornaments, all the time watching us, testing us to see what we'd do. We got up to go over and stop him, but just then his mother leaped up and grabbed him, threw him on the couch, and quite literally sat on him. In fact, throughout the appointment she had been threatening to do so: "If you aren't good I'm gonna have to sit right on top of you!" And that's exactly what she ended up doing. It was the only way she could control her child.

A week later she came back with her child, her husband and her dog. We all went out to a training area to discuss the dog, and again the child was being a non-stop little brat. He didn't want us to work with the dog at all, and was doing everything he could to get everyone to pay attention only to him. He kept grabbing his mother's leg so she couldn't walk, competing with the dog for everyone's attention. The mother kept telling him "No," and pushing the little boy away. For his part, the little kid kept grabbing her and hitting her, refusing to be ignored. All this time she kept threatening him: "If you're not good, I'm gonna put you in the trunk of the car!"

If we didn't get the kid under control we'd never be able to get around to talking about the dog. "Let's do some dog training here," we said. "We've learned in dog training that, in cases like this, ignored behavior actually goes away. It'll get worse at first, but it will go away."

When the kid was out of earshot, we said: "Let's try this. we want you to totally ignore him. Absolutely ignore him. He'll hit you and grab you and do anything else he can to get your attention, because he knows he'll get it. You always give him a reaction when he does so. You've been very accommodating to him, so he knows he's got you where he wants you," we said, a little nervous that they might think we were way overstepping our bounds. "Try it. Just totally ignore him. It won't be easy, but it'll help. You'll see."

They did as we asked and sure enough, the child continued to misbehave, and his attempts to distract his mother escalated. we kept encouraging her to ignore him, but it was hard for her because he was really getting at her and because she was so accustomed to reacting to him when he acted like this. The father sat quietly off to the side, doing nothing. He didn't say a word the whole time; he just watched. That really made us nervous. Finally, after what must have seemed like an eternity to the mother, the child understood that he wasn't going to get his mother's attention so he turned around and went off to the side and started to play by himself. After that, we could discuss their dog.

As they were leaving, we couldn't help but say to the mother: "We have to ask you something. Would you really have put him in the trunk of the car like you were threatening to do?"

It's the only way I can make him sit!

"Of course not!" she said, a little worried that we thought she might be some kind of monster.

"Then why in the world did you threaten it? If you're not going to carry out a threat, you're just teaching him that you don't mean what you say. You're actually teaching him to disregard you."

At that point we realized we'd probably stuck our necks out just a bit too far. The funny thing was, after we said that, the father came over to us, shook hands and said, "Thank you! Thank you!" Their child's behavior was noticeably improved the rest of our session together, so we guess the father had caught on and was grateful for this extra instruction. But, the fact of the matter is that it wasn't extra instruction at all. As it turned out, they were having the same kind of leadership problems with their dog. It didn't really matter if we started working on the child or the dog, but the child seemed to be in more urgent need of the training than the dog at that moment. Leaders lead, and they have to constantly communicate to the rest of the pack that they're in charge.

Leaders expect their commands to be obeyed, not ignored for a certain amount of time until the boiling point is reached. When you give your child to the count of three to do something: "One...Two...Three!" when does he respond? If it's when you say "Three," you're teaching him to ignore "One" and "Two." People do this all the time. They say "I told you not to do that." "Now don't do that again!" "Johnny, I told you before to stop that!" "Johnny!!" The more you let it go, the more you teach your child just how much he or she can really get away with. And, when their behavior is allowed to escalate like this, they reach a boiling point and blow up at them. If Johnny knew that you were serious the first time, he would have stopped the first time. This also happens with your dogs. You need to impress on them that when you say "No," you mean "No," the first time. A dog who ignores his owner when a truck is bearing down on him won't have a second chance to obey when he feels like it, or after his owner gives the command three or four times. Don't teach your kids to disregard you by making empty threats. That just results in empty authority.

Once you start teaching this kind of disrespect—yes, you're teaching them to disrespect you if you fail to take on the responsibility of leadership—you'll probably start seeing it right away. Once your dog is trained, that is, once he demonstrates his understanding of a particular command like sit, you can rest assured he's smart enough to remember that command and the appropriate response to it. If your dog doesn't respond to a command after this point, several things may be going on. One is that he's just too excited or distracted at the moment to give you his full attention: that squirrel just made an insulting gesture at him and, by golly, that squirrel's going to pay for it! However, if there are no obvious distractions and your dog doesn't respond to a known command, it may be because he doesn't recognize you as pack leader. Maybe he thinks of himself as pack leader. If that's the case, he's really saying: "Sorry, but I don't respect your so-called authority enough to work with you, and I will not submit to you. I will not sit or lie down for you because I do not respect you." Under these circumstances, respect for your authority must be established because simply attempting to practice prior commands and training exercises with him won't fix the problem. He'll simply continue to ignore you because he's been taught to. Again, why shouldn't he ignore you if you refuse to take charge?

"Turn off the TV, Honey. It's time for bed."

"Noooo! I don't wanna!"

"Just a few more minutes then..."

Who's in charge around here, anyway?

If you refuse to establish or consistently communicate your authority, you're setting yourself up for all kinds of behavior problems with both your dog and your kids. Take Attila, for example. We visited a client at his home who had a little Pomeranian named Attila. The owner himself was a big guy, pushing three hundred pounds and rock solid. Attila, on the other hand, was maybe four or five pounds, tops. Believe or not, this fellow was telling us that Attila was controlling his life; that this little Pomeranian could be quite nasty to him and bite. We were sitting there, listening to this guy go on about how vicious Attila was, thinking "Uh huh. Right." There's this little dog running around the living roomchasing a ball and being cute, and here's the guy who looks like a linebacker telling us that Attila was controlling his life.

Our disbelief must have shown on our faces because the man finally said, "You really don't believe me, do you?"

"Well, it's not that we don't believe you," we said, careful not to dismiss him out of hand, "but, well, we haven't seen any problems with him the whole time we've been here."

"You want me to demonstrate?"

Uh, oh. Little alarms started going off.

"I don't want anybody to get hurt," we said cautiously, "but we wouldn't mind seeing what you interpret as bad behavior."

There was a little dog crate in the room, so the man said, "Attila, get in your crate." At that, Attila turned, looked at him and growled.

Please, Attila...*open the door!*

"You haven't seen anything yet," he told us. He walked over and tapped on the crate, saying, "Come on, get in here!" At that, Attila simply flew at him. That little dog was going to tear him to pieces! Attila was well named.

We managed to get Attila settled down enough to go on with our discussion. The fellow then started to describe his problems when he wanted to go to bed: Attila would jump up on the bed first and wouldn't move over enough for him to lie down. It took a great deal of persuasion just to get into bed each night. Eventually, he could get in bed, but then Attila would curl up next to his back, and if the fellow moved at all during the night, Attila would bite him.

We assured Atilla's owner that we could work him through this behavior through training, and we took Attila back to the Academy with us. Unfortunately, even after the training was successful, Atilla's owner was still afraid he might revert to his old ways. At that point, Attila was quite well behaved, but the man still lived in fear of him. Shortly after Atilla's training was completed, we ran into an older woman who was looking for a small, active dog. We told her we had just the thing for her, but we also warned her that Attila was one tough little dog. The woman, about 70, said, "I'm damn tough, too!" Somehow we couldn't help but feel that those two were going to get along fine together. The woman got her dog, and Attila got someone who could take charge of him: Attila had found his leader.

As it turned out, she called us a year later and told us: "This is just the most delightful little dog. I can't believe that anyone could ever have had any problems with him." They made a perfect match of personalities: She was a no-nonsense top dog, and Attila was finally released from the burden of having to run the pack. If Atilla's original owner had accepted the responsibility of being pack leader right from the start, there would never have been a problem.

Just like the woman who had to sit on her child, you can be dominated by your kids if you don't establish respect for your authority, or if you teach your kids that your authority is just an "iffy" sort of thing. If you don't take the responsibility of being the pack leader, or if you fail to be consistent in insisting on respect for your authority, your kids will dominate us just as surely as Attila dominated his first owner.

How *do* you communicate respect for your authority? For starters, you communicate confidence in your authority. You do this through your bearing, your postures, your tone of voice and the decisiveness you exhibit in making choices and giving commands.

You'd be surprised how much your posture and body language says to others, especially your dog. You know to stand up straight with your shoulders back when you're introduced to the person conducting a job interview—it's the posture of confidence and strength. And, you all know what kinds of messages of weakness or carelessness you send when you slouch and slump. Those kinds of postures are screaming their messages, just like a raised fist does, or an open, extended palm-up gesture. Body language is important. Dogs notice your nonverbal behavior, just like they notice the body language of other dogs. Just as in canine packs, as leaders you need to occupy the highest ground. Leaders are quite literally top dog. When you exercise your leadership around your dog, you should literally stand up to him. When you're not showing your authority through your posture, don't expect to be respected. If you're lying on the carpet watching TV or kneeling in front of your dog you're not demonstrating a position of leadership and authority. You are literally coming down to the level of the underlings in the pack. Imagine going through a training session with your dog while lying on a couch. You're much more effective when you're standing up and facing your dog while giving commands.

Certain basic commands also drive home the idea of leadership through body language. *Down* is used as a signal to the dog that you are the leader. Putting your dog in the down position is a way of telling him that you're in command. Height is might, and when he's down and you're up, you're the one in charge. A dog who is reluctant to learn the down response may actually be struggling with you about who's really in charge. Certain breeds like Shar-Peis and Chow Chows are notorious about being difficult to get into a down position. These are stout, dominant dogs who don't take kindly to someone coming along and telling them to assume an inferior position or be submissive.

The tone of voice you adopt when training and giving commands is also important to whether or not your dog sees you as pack leader. As a leader, your voice should be calm and confident, not high-pitched or whiny. How do *you* react to someone with a whiny voice? When giving commands or just talking to your dog, use your normal voice and don't end the command in a questioning tone. Don't drag out the vowels in a command word as if you weren't sure of yourself: "Bozo, sit. No, Bozo, siiiiiiit."

The confidence in your voice has to be matched by confidence in your bearing and the confidence you have in yourself. If you're trying to get your dog to feel comfortable about a particular situation, but you're not comfortable with it yourself, it'll show, and your dog will pick up on that uncertainty and be uncertain himself. If you leave the house every day anxious about leaving your dog home by himself, he senses it. Soon he'll be worried about being alone, too. If you make a big deal about telling him that everything will be all right once you're gone, he's going to sense your concern and start to get concerned himself. Dogs are more sensitive to your moods and anxieties than you might think. Instead of passing them along to your dog—or your other kids—be calm and confident in your actions and your decisions.

Leaders lead in everything. That goes for not only setting up the rules, but also in following them. You have to be consistent with your kids in both abiding by the rules yourself, and in insisting that they're followed by your pack at all times. Leaders expect their commands to be obeyed, not just some of the time, but always. When you don't insist on obedience all the time, or if you break the rules yourself, you're teaching your dog and your kids that the rules don't always apply. In other words, you're teaching them that you're not always the leader and that the rules can be discarded. When you start down that road, you can expect your leadership and your authority to be ignored.

Leaders lead, and that means going first through doors into rooms, cars, and out of the house. Leaders decide who gets what. Never allow the dog to make the decision about what is his. That goes for the bed, the couch, a particular place in the house, your shoes, and even dog toys. If your dog growls at you when you take a toy away from him, you've got leadership problems. When you play tug-of-war with something with your dog, better make sure that you win that little game. Otherwise, he just took something from you and got away with it. Who's top dog now?

Leaders also create respect for their authority by inspiring trust in other pack members. Both your children and your dogs need to feel that you would never place them in dangerous situations. If your kids wander out into the street during playtime, you haul them back in and explain the danger to them and that you're looking out for them. You steer your dogs around fast water when you cross the stream and you don't compel them into situations that needlessly endanger them. They learn from you that your decisions can be trusted to act in their best interests. This kind of trust is usually the result of their long-term exposure to your own confident actions and decisions.

Trust is also created by getting your dog and your kids to believe that you are constantly watching them, both to protect them and to correct them if necessary.

Leaders teach other pack members to respect their authority by correcting transgressions against the rules of the pack. You should know right now that the corrections we use in our training are never intended as a form of physical punishment. You always get better results from positive reinforcement and encouragement than you do from any form of abuse. Do you really think your kid will get better in math if you yell at her and tell her how stupid she is when she brings home a poor mark on her report card? Think it might be better to work with her on her math instead? Maybe it would be more productive to establish rules about study habits and work periods after dinner when the pack leaders are around to supervise and encourage a positive work ethic? The same is true with your dog. You won't do any good with your dog by simply putting a leash on him and jerking his head off for half an hour during training sessions. You're trying to teach the dog something after all, not break him.

You should understand that leadership and dominance are two very different things. Leadership is about teaching and going first; it's about mutual respect and establishing your authority through rules and your own constancy and consistency—something your dog and your kids can trust in and rely on. The parent who leads poorly, who is inconstant and inconsistent, finds that transgressions are allowed to reach the boiling point of tolerance. Then, suddenly, explosively, the parent snaps and asserts his/her dominance over the children. Since no respect or trust has been established, the only way this dominance can be asserted is physically: "I'm bigger than you, so you will do as I say!" You might create obedience through fear this way, but you'll never have the respect of your pack.

We know people who train their dogs through fear tactics. It's absurd. What sort of respect do you think you get from doing so? You can inspire fear in someone else, but you'll never get respect from doing so, and you'll only get a mechanical obedience in the end, not the enthusiasm that's built on respect and trust. Imagine someone holding a gun to your head. You might do what they want out of fear, but would you respect that person? Admire them? Do what they want because you look up to them? Not a chance. In fact, you probably despise them for their cruelty, and the first chance you get you're going to pay them back for it. Compare that to the way you respond to someone you respect and admire. You'd do anything for them, anytime.

When your leadership is respected and when you're consistent with your kids about what the rules are and when and how they are to be obeyed, then corrections are only a potential. Once the rules are known, then you give your kids a choice: either accept my authority or be corrected for it. And, corrections *will* be handed out, make no mistake, especially in the early stages of training as part of saying to kids that you mean what you say.

Assuming responsibility of being a leader helps you avoid physical dominance. Leaders make the decisions, and in doing so they help to create focus for the pack and remove confusion. A confused child or dog is going to have a hard time being obedient. When you take charge with them, you're clearing the way for obedience.

A client taking our basic obedience training class told us that she didn't believe in saying no to her child because it would damage his self-esteem. To her, the word "no" implied punishment and generated negative feelings. This attitude carried over to the way she tried to train her dog. Without any means to control her dog verbally, this kind-hearted woman was forced to resort to violence, physically yanking and jerking her poor dog's head in an attempt to gain some control over him. As a result, her dog was agitated and confused. He didn't know what he was supposed to be doing, so he couldn't possibly please her.

It might seem a bit strange to say it, but challenges to your leadership should actually be expected, even if you're a good leader. That's because changes in yourself, in the pack structure, or in other members of the pack generally inspire pack members to see if anything has changed with the leader or the leader's rules, even if you've been a good, consistent leader all along. Sometimes these changes can't be helped; they're natural and you just have to deal with them. Maybe you've even thought about changes that might come along for the pack in advance, but you can't always know how they're really going to affect you and the rest of the pack. You *know* that your child or your puppy is going to become a teenager someday, but it's not always possible to anticipate just what that's going to involve for the family as a unit. On the other hand, sometimes the changes that come are unlooked-for and come as a big surprise to everyone. Whenever changes occur in the pack, challenges to leadership are likely going to happen.

In canine packs, anything that happens to the leader is likely going to bring about a challenge to the *alpha's* right to lead. For example, if the *alpha* is getting old and feeble or is injured or becomes ill, another dog in the pack might want to challenge his ability to look after the pack's welfare successfully. The same is true with your pack at home.

We have a client who has had many of her dogs with us in the past. She's been a great leader over the years, really trustworthy and on top of things, and always looking out for the best interests of the whole pack at home. Now she's at the Academy with a new dog, but things have changed in her leadership: she's just had some serious back problems—surgery and a lengthy convalescence—and her dogs are starting to ignore her. It's nothing she could help. And even though she's been a good leader and parent all along, the challenges are starting to come in anyway. She knows she's going to have to be firm to get through this until she's fully back on her feet and able to demonstrate her authority once again.

Marriage, childbirth and divorce bring changes to the pack. Someone new is brought in and your dog or your child may challenge this new person's role, or challenge the pack leadership as a way of reaffirming his old place in the pack. A dominant dog will challenge out of a desire to take over, but even a less dominant dog will do so to reaffirm its position to rest easy about the new pack structure. Divorce changes the dynamics of the pack. This can be disturbing for you parents left in charge, because you may find out that the rest of the pack never really considered you the pack leader after all. All of a sudden you find out that you were never thought of as top dog in the first place. Challenges to your leadership are going to start coming in then, and you must establish your leadership as fast as possible: "But mom never had us eat broccoli before!" "We're eating broccoli *now*." Both your kids and your dog will want to re-evaluate the pack's structure and its leadership to see if anything has changed.

Changes for pack members don't need to be as drastic or dramatic as a serious illness or a divorce for potential challenges to your leadership to emerge. Even something as simple and harmless as moving into a new house can cause a challenge to your authority. Rules are markers of constancy and comfort found in routine and expectations. When you move into a new home, the routine for the pack might be disrupted at first. Pack members may feel uprooted from everything, even the old rules. If that happens, then leadership has to reinforce the idea that just because the locale has changed, the rules have not.

Changes in the pack, for any reason, require that you have a good, strong foundation for obedience to your authority already in place. If that foundation isn't there, then the changes that come along will disrupt everything, and it'll be much harder for you to establish your authority afterwards. And, when the changes come, consistency and constancy are going to be vital to maintaining that leadership.

In the end, leadership is everything. It's the basis for any undertaking with your kids or your dogs. Without being the leader, you're not going to get very far with either of them. Being a good parent means being a good leader. It's a big responsibility, but it's necessary if you want your kids or your dogs to be both happy and obedient. Building a solid foundation for your leadership is the best thing you can do for all the members of your pack.

Chapter 4
Building a Foundation

Being a good parent is all about leadership. A fair bit of being a leader is teaching the rules: the benefits of following them, the consequences of ignoring them, what will be tolerated and what won't, and much more. Everything you do and say, and many things you don't, is part of this education. This is an on-going process—a constant thing—in which all your words and actions get picked up and filed away by your kids. When you lead, you're also teaching, and you need to be careful how you go about it.

Much can and does happen in the lives of your kids, and the result is that it's just about impossible to anticipate every situation that might come along. You can't expect to teach your kids in advance how they should react to every little thing. Because of that, you need to build a solid foundation for their behavior. This foundation must be so strong that no matter what happens, you will all be able to cope. This foundation is built by getting control over your kids from the very beginning, and by mastering some of the basics of control through your leadership. These basics involve structure, generalization and consistency.

Structure

By structuring, we mean that as pack leader you establish what the rules are and then follow them. A structure is a solid thing—structuring is establishing a solid set of rules. They are the guidelines for how you will interact with your dog. When these rules are established and insisted on, confidence in your ability as a leader is confirmed.

An important part of any set of rules for obedience is constancy. Constancy is important for at least two reasons. First, insisting on obedience is like repeating a lesson over and over until you're sure that your student has gotten it down for good and will never forget it. It's a way of teaching the process of obedience. Second, as you teach your student, you reinforce the idea that you are always the pack leader, not just part of the time, and that the rules are in effect at all times unless you say otherwise.

One of the most important things we do at the Academy is train the owners of a dog. There's no such thing as bringing your dog in to be fixed by training and then whisking him home to live happily ever after. It doesn't work that way. You have to be a part of your dog's training and obedience; in fact, you have to be the biggest part of your dog's obedience, because you're the one who has to live with him all the time, not us. As a result, we have to train the dog owners because they need to know how to train their dogs once they graduates from our Academy. That may seem a bit strange: Didn't he get trained here? Why should you need to train him any more? The fact is, you're training your dog constantly, whether you want to or not, a hundred times a day, and you need to learn how to go about doing this training effectively.

When we tell people they have to train their dogs 100 times a day, we either get a blank stare or an anguished response: "You mean I've got to spend that much time every day working with my dog? You can't be serious! I don't have that kind of time to work with him! I've got a job, you know. That's why I brought him here in the first place!" The reason people get so upset when we tell them they need to train their dogs 100 times a day is that they picture putting leashes on their dogs and working with them for 15 or 20 minutes. To them, that's training the dogs. However, any time you interact with your dog—any time at all— you're training him, for better or for worse.

Imagine coming home from work and your dog greeting you at the door. He's excited to see you, and a little too rambunctious for your work-frazzled brain, so you say, "Bozo, sit." He sits, so you say, "Good sit, Bozo," pet him and proceed to hang up your coat and get dinner going. The whole transaction took about three seconds. That's training your dog. You just asked him to sit when he would have preferred to jump all over you, so you just trained him to obey when he really wasn't in the mood for it.

Let's look at that same situation from another angle. You walk in the door and tell Bozo to sit, but instead he jumps all over you. You laugh at his playfulness and pet him, telling him what a sweet dog he is. You just trained him in that three-second span that it's perfectly acceptable for him to greet people like that. If you tell him to sit and he bounds over to you for affection and you give it to him, you've just trained him again, this time that commands from the pack leader are really only to be obeyed when he feels like it. That's training.

You're teaching your dog constantly, whether you realize it or not. The same is true with your kids. If you teach them that a certain kind of behavior must be maintained at the dinner table, but don't insist on the same behavior at the picnic table during the family reunion, you're teaching them that the rules only apply at certain times and in certain places. Being a parent is a full-time job, whether or not you wish it were otherwise. When you're with your kids or your dog, you're constantly teaching them. You've got a big choice to make. Will you accept the heavy responsibility of leadership and reinforce positive behavior all the time, or will you only take on that role here and there when you really feel like it? Because you're training constantly, if you set aside your insistence on obedience, even for a little while, you're actually training disobedience, whether you want to or not.

Setting up the rules for obedience for your two- and four-legged kids takes different forms. Among canines in the wild, the pack leader marks the pack's territory by urinating at its boundaries. That's not practical for humans, so you do it in other ways, either by showing your kids the territory or by correcting them when they go out-of-bounds. Territory is a big deal. Territory is what belongs to you; it's your place, and its boundaries mark off what is yours and what is not. The boundaries also mark what's safe and what's not. Pack leaders don't allow pack members to set up territory for themselves—that's the leader's privilege—and they don't allow pack members to cross outside the territory because that's when trouble starts. If you step over that boundary, you find yourself on somebody else's turf. You might allow your dog to feel as if he's got a right to challenge intruders on the pack's turf, like the yard, but you sure don't want him to jump the hedge and bite the neighbor in a mistaken attempt to protect the pack's territory. You don't want your little kids playing in the street, either, so the pack's territory ends at the sidewalk. You step over that boundary and the pack leader is going to have something to say about it.

It's important to set up territory for your dog. There are practical reasons for doing this, such as housetraining issues which we'll get to later, but establishing territory is something that pack leaders do, and as such territory is a mandate of authority. Setting up the rules for territory is a way of exercising your leadership and of setting up rules. If you don't do this, your dog will do it himself, and then his behavior becomes dependent on his own rules.

For example, does your dog like to be in the kitchen? Lots of dogs do. That's where the food is, after all. If you let your dog set up the kitchen as his territory, then at the very least he's always going to be underfoot when you're there. He may also be aggressive about just who goes in there and who doesn't. After all, it's his kitchen. The same is true with getting up on the couch or the bed. That's the high ground—the place for leaders—and if he takes over there your leadership is being infringed upon. Leaders set up the territory because it is their right to do so. Don't let your dog establish his own territory. Territory is a possession, and whether it's a place or a thing, leaders decide who gets what. Like Attila's first owner, you may find that getting into bed each night is an on-going battle.

You set the tone for everything with your dogs and your kids, including work and playtime. You initiate play with your dogs and kids. If there's work to be done, then, by golly, play is going to have to wait. During training sessions with your dog, set the mood for it. If your dog begins the session by being frantic about it and you get frantic yourself, then he just set the tone for the session, not you.

You establish the groundrules for your dog in everything, even eating and sleeping, just like you do with your other kids. You expect them to be at the dinner table at a certain time and in bed at a certain time. You are top dog in everything, and the top dog makes all the rules.

Above anything else, creating a structured life for both your dog and your kids is a way of laying down a foundation for behavior to be followed at all times. It is also a way of saying you care. Dogs require structuring in their lives to feel comfortable about where they stand in the pack and to have confidence that the pack leader is leading and all is well.

Believe it or not, this takes a lot of pressure off your dog and makes him a calmer, happier dog to live with. He's got no worries because the pack leader has everything under control. Now that he knows what's expected of him, he just has to follow the rules and the pack runs smoothly. What could be better?

Generalization

In training, the term *generalization* implies that the same command will mean the same thing, regardless of time of day, location, the person giving the command, the presence of a reward, the situation, or anything else. What this means is that you expect obedience always, in any place or any situation. You apply the command word in every environment and under every condition until your dog understands exactly what that word means and that an appropriate response is required, always. You want to get to the point in educating your dogs in which you can expect obedience in any situation, not just during nice, calm, controlled training sessions. There's no question that it's nice to have your dog come running to you with a big grin on his face after you've given the come command during a training session, but it's even more important for him to obey that command when he's sitting out in the street with a speeding truck headed his way, or when he has an intense desire to investigate that porcupine.

Concepts like *always* are not clear to a dog. Early on in our careers as trainers, we discovered that if a dog was worked each day at the same time and in the same location, he would be a bit rusty with his responses to commands if his parents visited at a time other than his normal training period. The dog seemed to think that the only time it was really necessary for him to obey was during those regularly scheduled work periods. When his parents visited, it was almost as if he was thinking: I don't have to do this. This is usually when I'm out playing with the other dogs. When are they going to let me go out and play?

Dogs are creatures of habit, just like people. Routine and ritual are as important to your dog as they are to a two-year-old child. This can be both good and bad. If you schedule training sessions for every Saturday afternoon in the back yard, the only time your dog is really going to work for you is Saturday afternoon in the back yard. The rest of the time he's going to feel like he can do what he pleases, because the rest of the time you don't actively work with him on obeying. That's another reason why training has to be a constant, on-going process, 100 times a day. The good thing about dogs being creatures of habit is that you can, with structure and consistency, generalize their learning so they get into the habit of obeying commands anytime.

Dogs and little kids don't see and understand things the way you do as adults. The passage of time and a change in locale create totally different situations to their way of thinking. Understanding this will help you see the need for generalization. Imagine yourself starting out your puppy's training with the simplest command, *sit*. Most dogs quickly learn this command because it's natural for them to sit and you can, in time, get them to associate doing so with the command word by saying "Good sit" whenever they sit. But, let's see how a dog's brain processes this learning during your early stages of working with him.

You're playing with your puppy on the kitchen floor and you decide to work on the command *sit*. You say sit and you help him into a sitting position, telling him "Good sit, Bozo!" After a few tries, your puppy is actually starting to sit on command. You're so proud of him. You're thinking of going and getting the video camera right now, just like you did when your child first started to stumble around without crawling. It's a heady moment. So, you pick him up and pack him off to the living room to show your spouse: Look what I've just taught our puppy to do." This is going to be great. You set your puppy down and with a big smile you say "sit," sort of dragging that "i" out for dramatic effect. As a response, your puppy wags his tail and saunters off in search of adventure. Wait a minute! This is awful! Your ego is involved and that little runt didn't do his sit. "You dumb dog. Get yourself over here right now and sit or I'll..."

There are a number of important things going on here, but one of the most important is that your puppy really doesn't have a clue yet as to what you're asking him to do. A few minutes ago, you were playing this really fun game with him way over there in the kitchen, and he noticed that you got really excited when he did something during the game. Now you're all cranky about something. What a grouch.

The fact is, he had no notion that there was any sort of connection between what you said and what he did. It was all just the give and take of the game you were playing. "Why is she so mad at me? What did I do?" The puppy can't figure out what's different about why you were so happy over there in the kitchen, but so angry in the living room. In fact, after a fairly good start, this word *sit* doesn't sound like so much fun anymore. Even as your puppy grows older, sit may only mean to sit when this or that is going on, or onlyduring a particular time of day, or only in certain places, unless that command is generalized. Your little kids are like that, too. If you tell little Suzy to stop playing with the vase, she probably will. Satisfied, you walk out of the room. Ten minutes later, you come back and Suzy's playing with the vase again. What the..? "Didn't I just tell you to stop playing with that vase?" This is a bit confusing for little Suzy. She did stop playing with the vase, just like you said, but that was then. Entire minutes have passed. Glaciers have come and gone since then. Suzy didn't realize that you meant stop playing with the vase until she's old enough to afford a Tiffany's of her own.

With your puppy, the word *sit*, and all his commands, will need to be generalized for him through constant training— again, in those little three-second bursts—in all kinds of environments and situations. He, and you, will need to keep on practicing until he can sit in the kitchen, the living room, the hallway, the driveway, the park or anyplace else. Pretty soon, you've got the word *sit* generalized to the point where your dog understands that it doesn't matter where you or he are, he sits when he hears that command.

We have clients bring their dogs to the Academy because they're having a particular problem and they want that particular problem fixed. What they're really looking for is a magic bullet: something that will seek out and affect only that particular problem without really touching anything else. Even though it's true that you sometimes have to put in extra effort with a particular problem your dog is having with his training, in most cases you really have to have a foundation for obedience established first. Once that's accomplished, commands and obedience can be generalized to cope with almost any situation.

Generalization negates the need to create thousands of commands to accommodate every new situation. As you'll see as you go along, you really only need to teach and generalize a handful of commands to be happy with your dog, even though he's quite capable of learning hundreds of them. For example, why try to come up with a command like "Do Not Chase The Cat" or "Do Not Eat The Azaleas" or "Do Not Scratch The Door," when you can teach and generalize a command like "Leave It," which is intended to turn your dog's attention away from any on-going or potential activity?

We had a client who came in with her dog for Basic Training. One of the commands he learned while he was there was "Leave It." When the training was complete, we drove him back to his owner's home. Later, we were all out in her back yard putting the dog through his paces. She was very impressed. Then she said, "Did he learn about not chasing people when they walk between the houses?" We both gave her a blank stare and said "What? You never told us there was any problem like that." At that, she burst into tears. "Oh, this is terrible! I'm going to be sued!"

"Wait a minute," we said. "Just because we haven't dealt with that specific problem doesn't mean that you don't have control over your dog."

"You don't understand," she wailed. "The situation is just terrible. Every time our neighbor..."

As luck would have it, along came the very man her dog had chased between houses. Naturally, the dog started out after him. We turned and said, "No! Leave it!" and the dog came back. "You see? It's not necessary to train for a specific situation. You only have to train the dog to obey basic commands at any time you want." To the client, it seemed like a miracle.

The idea of generalization is to have obedience at all times, not just here or there, or during particular situations. We have people come to the Academy with dogs who are so well trained that it makes you wonder what in the world they're doing there in the first place. They tell their dogs sit and they sit, so why are they looking for professional help? They're looking for help because they really don't have control over their dogs. Problems with behavior are not necessarily similar to having a problem with getting your dog to learn a specific command. You can have a dog who is quite well trained, but not have any real control over him.

Some years ago, we invited a woman to stay with us while she was in town for a dog-obedience competition. She was one of the top competition obedience trainers in the country, and her dog was one of the highest-scoring competition obedience dogs. During the competition, her dog scored 199 and 1/2 points out of a possible 200. That was some dog, and he easily won the competition that day. We were looking forward to her staying with us, because it's always a treat to be around a top-flight, well-trained dog.

Amazingly, though, when she brought her dog to our place, he behaved so badly that she had to confine him to his crate. He was all over the place, and she had absolutely no control over him outside the competition ring. That was one ring-smart dog, but he didn't make a very pleasant companion. His owner had obviously trained him for obedience in only a single situation, the ring, and outside that ring he was a maniac. The human analogy to this situation is having children attend a very strict, private school and obey the letter of the law down to its last detail while they're on the school grounds. Once they're off the premises, they run amok. They're out of the *ring* and out of control. If the school teacher can get them to be well-mannered at school, how come they misbehave when you're at church? Generalization intends to create obedience in any situation or setting.

We had a St. Bernard named Kitten come in because she had the tendency to get a bit aggressive when a lot of people were around. She didn't like all the activity going on around her because it made her nervous. She was a big dog, and any sort of bad temper in dogs that size can be disaster for those around them. She went through a month of our board-and-train program, and we were able to handle her aggressiveness. However, Kitten's owners were still nervous about how she'd react to a particular situation.

They weren't secure with the concept of generalization, and it worried them that they might lose control over her if she was faced with something new. They were giving a big party at their house and wanted to show off Kitten, but to their way of thinking, Kitten hadn't taken a class on party training, so they were nervous about her behavior. As a result, they called and asked if we'd escort Kitten to the big party. This was still early in our career as a trainers, and we wanted to see how our training was being applied in the family's home, so we accepted the invitation.

As it turned out, we had a wonderful time at the party, even though Kitten hogged all the attention. What a flirt. Her parents were surprised to discover what a debutante she had become, and they also found out that Kitten's basic training had been a class on party training after all. In the end, Kitten's training was well on its way, but her parents still had a lot to learn about the day-to-day application of that training.

Generalization also involves the idea of obedience from any and all authority figures. When we have a dog in for the month-long board and train at the Academy, we'll schedule the parents to come in for nonworking visits. This means that a trainer works the dog for the parents, but the parents aren't allowed to work him themselves. This is an effective way to get the dog to obey while he's distracted, because his parents are there and he's really excited to see them. He has to continue to obey, even though he's so excited. This is also an effective way to generalize obedience as a way of overcoming the dreaded Babysitter Syndrome.

Have you ever babysat? Everyone should do it as a crash course on leadership skills and generalizing authority. Corporate seminars should teach leadership skills by sending clients out for a week of babysitting. If you've ever done any babysitting, you've no doubt given your tiny charge a command and then were faced with the old, "I don't have to do what you say. You're not my mom/dad!" How you respond to that little package of defiance is a good indication of your leadership skills. If your response is, "Well, I, no...but...," you fail. But, if your response is something more along the lines of, "That's right, I'm not your 'mom'...I'm the one in charge who's telling you to get your little rump in bed right now," then you're on the right track.

It's true: As a babysitter you're not his parent, but that doesn't mean that you're not in charge. mom and dad transferred that authority to you, and they're counting on you to get things done while they're gone. You're the one in charge now, and that authority needs to be recognized by those in your temporary care. Their obedience has to be to anyone who's in charge, not just mom and dad. When mom and dad come home, they're going to have to have a little talk with the defiant one about obeying the rules even when they're not around. That's what those nonworking visits do. The trainer is giving the dog commands and the dog is often shouting, "You're not my mom! She's right over there and just wait 'til she..." But mom is not interceding on the dog's

Kitten learns party manners.

behalf; in fact, mom is just calmly watching as the dog is expected to obey. Mom and dad are not there to get their dog off the hook after all. Obedience is for always, regardless of which authority figure is giving the commands.

Generalization is a process of foundation building. It underlies obedience from your dogs, or your kids, in any situation. If you can generalize commands, then no matter what happens, you and your dog and kids will be prepared. On the surface, generalization seems simple enough: you just keep working on obedience to a particular command in lots of different situations.

However, as you'll see when we talk about training, it's more complicated than that. It's also a process that includes concerns other than just working on a command in different situations. People often want to jump ahead to a particular problem behavior in their kids or their dogs without doing all the other necessary things that make solving a particular problem possible.

It's a little like saying, "I'm not very happy about the way you're handling the calculus I'm trying to teach you," even though you haven't bothered to teach addition yet. If you say, "I don't care if my dog doesn't sit when I ask him to, and I don't care if he goes down when I want him to, I just want him to stop barking," then you're unclear on the most important element in training your dog. But, if you mean sit when you say sit, and when you mean down when you say down, then stop barking means stop barking. It's just one more step in the education process. It's all a part of generalizing obedience.

Generalizing is more than just working toward obedience in a variety of situations, it's creating obedience always, and that's different. Just like with the babysitter, even things like who's giving the commands needs to be generalized. We've had people bring their dogs into the Academy who expressed their reservations about our training, because they were worried that once they got home their dogs wouldn't obey them, just the trainer who had taught them. At the Academy, we have different trainers working the same dog. We also work the dog in different locations and at different times during the day to ensure that the idea of obedience-always is what's being driven home.

You might be surprised to know that it's important to generalize the manner in which you give a command. Usually, during a training exercise in the back yard, your tone of voice is fairly constant. It doesn't seem to matter what your personality is like during training, you always seem to stay on an even keel with your voice during those formal sessions.

During those sessions it's fairly typical that, when you give a command and have it obeyed by your dog, you're up-beat with your voice. That's good for praising your dog's accomplishments, but the command itself should be taught using a variety of tones. If you're out in the yard and singing come as a command, your dog might not have the slightest notion of what you're asking when you roar *come* as he's sidling up to that porcupine.

If you're looking for obedience, happiness or just plain satisfaction that everything around you is going like it should, you've got to work to build that foundation first. You can't try to stick a brick in to plug a hole when there's nothing holding up the wall in the first place. Similarly, you can't expect to solve some particular behavior problem with your dog or your kids if you haven't yet created a general foundation for good behavior. Generalization works to create that foundation, and your leadership is the mortar that holds together what you build on that foundation. Negligence, however, tears down any structure over time. You've got to be vigilant; you've got to be on your toes all the time, or else the walls will start falling down around you.

Consistency

I hope you haven't set the book down right now and run out to try to get your dog to sit all over the place, saying sit to him in four languages and using a false mustache for good measure. Generalizing commands is a wonderful thing, but building that foundation for obedience involves more than just taking your dog out for training sessions all over the countryside and talking to him using all the falsetto and vibrato that your voice and imagination can muster. Before you start trying to command obedience and consistency in your dog, you've got to master those things yourself. If you want consistency in your dog, or you kids, you have to be consistent yourself. Consistency is essential for both good leadership and obedience.

With canine packs, there are two *alphas*, the male and the female. This is still often the case with your pack at home these days. If that's the case with your family, then as pack leaders you need to present a unified front. There can't be any, "Ask your mother," or "Ask your father," sort of thing. Both pack leaders have to be clear on what the rules are so that there is consistency. If there isn't this unified front among the leadership, you're going to start teaching your kids disobedience because you're going to teach them that it's possible to go over your head to some other authority.

Has that ever happened to you during your visit to grandma's house? You tell your child that she can't do something and the next thing you know, she's gone and asked grandma, who is willing to pour warm syrup all over her little precious fingers if asked to. The leadership just got blown out of the water by a bigger ship. How do you countermand the leader's leader? You sit down and have a long talk with grandma about what the rules are and that the rules get obeyed no matter what. You get things straight about who's leader of your pack. This isn't always a pleasant thing to do, but it's got to be done if you're going to be consistent about obedience.

You have to be consistent about what the rules are, or else one of you is going to be teaching that the behavior that the other one disapproves of, is actually okay. As a part of being consistent about the rules, you've also got to be consistent about discipline and making corrections of undesirable behavior. None of this you-wait-until-your-father-gets-home excuse. No one parent should be forced to be the heavy while the other one gets to be the fountain of affection and acquiescence for the family. When you do that, you're telling the pack that if they want to get what they want, they just have to go to the proper leader, the good one. Rules and obedience are only going to matter if the pack understands that the *alphas* both feel the same way about things. The pack has to follow the rules, because there's nobody around to get them off the hook.

Consistency is also constancy, and we can't teach you that. Constancy is desire; it's the notion of having a goal and sticking to it. It's hard, especially when you're tired or when the circumstances make it inconvenient for you, but when you're not teaching obedience, you're actually teaching disobedience. You're on the phone and the dogs are barking at the cat across the street. You tell them to be quiet, but that cat is really being insulting and they just have to tell him all about his ancestors and his offspring. To the person on the other end of the line you say, "Excuse me, I'll be right back," and you go and inform your dogs that be quiet means BE QUIET.

Obedience is for always. If you can't be constant, then you can't be consistent, and that means that you can forget about your leadership and about the prospect of generalizing the obedience that is dependent on that leadership.

Building a foundation for obedience depends on a number of things: your leadership, your willingness to teach and reinforce positive behavior, your constancy and consistency, and the time you put in to generalize your dog's behavior. It's a lot to keep in mind, and maybe a lot for some people to keep up with, but it's really not as complicated as it might sound at first. Much of building a solid foundation for obedience is attitude and desire. You've got to want to teach positive behavior in your dog, or your child, or else it'll soon become difficult to remain constant and consistent in your training. If you need motivation for finding that desire in yourself so you can build and maintain the proper attitude for being a good leader and parent, just keep thinking about the alternatives. There's an awful lot of potential Attilas out there, and not all of them are running around on four legs.

Chapter 5
Training Through Leadership

What is training, anyway? For one thing, training isn't just a process, it's also an end-product. It's not only working for something, it's having something in the end—something that won't go away. And the end product you work for is obedience. Training means teaching your dog, or your child, to obey even when he's not in the mood to do so. It essentially comes down to the idea that although he might not want to sit now, since you're calling the shots, he's going to sit anyway. And, your dog will do so, despite any distractions.When sit means to sit—anytime and every time—then you have successfully trained your dog to sit. To train successfully for this kind of obedience, you have to make good use of your position as pack leader, and you have to remain both constant and consistent in your training if you hope to achieve the proper level of generalization that ensures obedience can be expected in any situation at any time.

Before you start any kind of training for obedience, you need to have a working vocabulary for training your dog, and you should also have a clear sense of what types of commands you're giving at any particular moment. Dogs don't understand the human language. As a result, you can choose any word you want to represent a particular command idea, as long as you're consistent about it. However, the kinds of commands you use, not the words themselves, and the responses you expect from those commands are understood by your dog in different ways. Because of that, you need to give a bit of forethought to the kinds of command/responses you're going to teach so you can understand how you're going to teach those commands in the first place.

Training Vocabulary

As a starting point, let's just run through a list of basic commands that can be generalized to adapt obedience to just about any situation. This is for the sake of understanding what these commands intend to create as a response. After you have a sense of what sort of things you need to teach your dog to create a foundation for obedience, then you can explore how these commands are taught and how you can avoid teaching disobedience while you're doing so.

SIT means for your dog to assume a sitting position. The hand signal that typically accompanies the verbal command is a raised hand, open flat, palm up, in front of and above your dog's head. This command is a bit trickier than you might think, even though it's probably the simplest of commands for a dog to master. You'll see some of the complications with this command later on.

WAIT is a useful command because it means for the dog to maintain his current station. This command is important in reinforcing your status as pack leader, because leaders go first in everything and only allow other pack members to proceed as the leader sees fit. You use this command when passing through doorways or preparing to get into or out of a car. In the dog's eyes the territory has changed. You actually give permission to your dog to pass through a doorway. This command can also be used to have your dog wait in a certain area or room. However, it is not intended for your dog to maintain a specific position, such as a sit or a down. It only requires that your dog wait for your release before he is able to cross a certain line, real or imaginary. This command can be a real life-saver when you and your dog are on opposite sides of a busy highway.

DOWN is the command you use to get a dog into a lying-down position. This command is *not* used to make your dog get down off something. As with so many other accompanying hand signals, the signal for down is a natural indication of a desired action: moving your hand downward in front of your dog; your dog should follow your hand to the ground. Take it slowly when teaching this command. It, too, is a signal of your status as pack leader because it requires your dog to take up an inferior or submissive position, and some dogs may be initially reluctant to place themselves in this position. It is also a position of some vulnerability, and you don't want your dog to be afraid when this command is given.

STAY is an absolute in comparison to a mere wait. When this command is given, the dog is expected to stay in the spot and position where he was placed, regardless of anything going on around him. While you can call your dog off a wait by simply telling him okay, you never call your dog off a stay. When this command is terminated, the dog is physically released by you. You walk over to him, praise him with a light pet and say okay. Wait is often a temporary thing, allowing you just the moment needed to pass through the door before your dog does, but stay is for more prolonged maintenance of a position.

DOWN STAY is just what it implies: your dog must stay in one place, but also maintain the down position. You often use this command during training sessions as a way of increasing a dog's attention span and to help him gain self-control and confidence, or as a way of establishing dominance. If a dog breaks from a down-stay then he must be returned to the previous position and do the down-stay again.

LEAVE IT seems to be a favorite command. The leave-it command requires that your dog turn his attention away from something. This command can be given while the dog is engaged in some action, or even if you have reason to believe that he *will* engage in an action. This command requires a physical response as an indication that his attention is no longer focused on what he was supposed to leave alone: he has to turn away from that thing.

This is one of those commands that, when generalized, alleviates the need for hundreds of commands to cope with specific situations. No need to have a don't-scratch or don't-eat-the-cat command when you've got a leave it in your repertoire. Keep in mind, however, that your dog may interpret leave it in a very temporary way. Your notion of time is likely going to be very different from his.

GO TO RUG is also a useful command when things get hectic and you'd like to avoid having a dog underfoot. This command is the dog's equivalent of doing a *time out* you might use with your child. You should get your dog a throw rug of some kind and put it in a safe place. When you want your dog to be in a specific place or simply to have him out of the way or calm down after some play, you have him go to his rug and wait or stay for awhile. Being on the rug is usually a good place for your dog, because in time he'll think of it as his special place and as such it's a comfortable place to be.

QUIET simply means to stop barking or whining. All corrections for this command should be made calmly but firmly, even though this is often the time you feel most like shouting yourself. (You don't want to sound as if you are barking also.) When your dog complies, give praise to reinforce the positive behavior.

DON'T PULL is a command used when walking your dog on a leash. Both of you, however, are responsible for maintaining a lack of tension on the leash. This means that while you will need to correct your dog for pulling, you will need to avoid doing so yourself.

GET/GO ON/GO AWAY are all different words for the same response, having your dog move away from you. This is more useful than you might think at first. There are times when you just need to have your dog out of your face, and it's important that he learns that the pack leader determines when affection or physical contact is made. When teaching this command, it's important that your dogs understand that you're not mad at him when sending him away. Praise his response, but remain adamant that you haven't changed your mind about where he is, even though you're praising him.

OFF means that your dog needs to get all four feet on the ground and off you, someone else, the furniture, or anything else. When teaching this command, don't pull or push your dog around. Let him do the work himself until he understands his job and how to do it.

GET HOME is another useful command, even if you've got a securely fenced yard. It's always a good idea for your dog to know what the boundaries are.

COME means to do just that: come to you. The emphasis with this command is the to-you part of it. When you're out walking your dog and you say come, it doesn't mean that your dog can come flying through your sphere of influence and then on to new adventures without a pause. It's always a bit frustrating to yell come out in the middle of a big field and have your dog come galloping toward you at the speed of light, only to whiz right past you and off into the wild blue yonder. The smile that you had on your face while he was approaching just naturally crumbles away as you realize that your dog thought come simply meant for you to pass the baton off to him so that he could thunder to the finish line. Come means to come right here and stand or sit in front of me until instructed otherwise.

This is just a sample of the variety of commands that your dog is capable of learning, but the ones listed here are the most useful for accommodating a range of potential obedience needs. When this short list of commands becomes generalized, you'll be surprised what kind of control you have over your dog and what kind of obedience you can command to cope with just about anything that comes along.

Command Types
Before you start to learn how to teach these commands, you need to understand that these and other commands are not all the same type. That is, not only are the expected responses from your dog different for each command, but how you go about teaching these commands is also going to be different depending on the command type. This is because your dog has a rather limited sense of the abstract. While some commands refer to a position in which your dog can be physically placed, other commands are more abstract and don't allow you to show the dog what you're driving at. In those instances, other teaching methods will be necessary.

There are three basic command types: conditioned, concrete and abstract. Conditioned and abstract commands cannot be taught through demonstration; they can only be reinforced with praise when the dog has initiated the action himself. Concrete commands, however, are ones that allow you to show the dog what you mean, and in these instances you attach a command word to those actions or responses as you're teaching them—as opposed to waiting for the dog to do something you approve of and then reinforcing that behavior through praise.

Conditioned Vocabulary? Good and No
The basis for conditioning commands, particularly abstract ones, requires that you make use of the words *good* and *no*, which can be thought of as the start-and-stop buttons on your dog. Good encourages and reinforces positive behavior and conditions that an action, or a

lack of one, is desirable. No is a signal to your dog to stop whatever he's doing and clear his mind for further instructions.

Conditioning is training that in many cases elicits a physiological response from the dog. It is Pavlovian conditioning. Russian physiologist Ivan Pavlov conditioned a number of dogs to begin salivating every time he rang a bell, because he associated the ringing of the bell with the giving of biscuits to his dogs. They started salivating because of the presence of the biscuit, but as time went by the dogs came to associate the coming of biscuits with the ringing of the bell. In the end, Pavlov only had to ring the bell to get his dogs to start salivating, because they understood that anytime that bell rang, the biscuit was on its way. He had effectively substituted one kind of stimulation for another. You can do the same thing with conditioned vocabulary. This is what happens when you condition your dogs through associating the word good with desirable behavior and the praise that it elicits.

Good. At the Academy, we have clients come in with their new puppies to have them evaluated for potential needs and to help new parents understand their puppies better. During these sessions, we start the conditioning process with the word good. Good is conditioned into every positive stimulus your dog experiences.

If your dog likes to have his back scratched or his ears rubbed or he likes a doggy biscuit, those are positive stimuli. When your dog experiences those things, you should be using the word good to accompany them, conditioning him to understand that good means something good is going on.

Most puppies respond to a belly rub by going into what looks like a semi-trance—belly-rubs feel good. Far from being in a trance, though, the little guy's mind is really quite receptive because he's calm and comfortable. All the time you're rubbing him say, very calmly and quietly: "Good. Isn't that good? That's good. That's really good." All through this the emphasis is placed on that quietly spoken good. There's no need for volume when using that word. Your dog's hearing is much better than yours. Calm and quiet is also good for a puppy.

This kind of conditioning actually evokes a state of mind in the dog completely separate from what your hands are doing. Good becomes a good feeling, not a signal for being rubbed. And, the more things that become associated with good, the more this word is associated with a general sense that all is well, and not with getting a treat or being petted. It becomes the start button for your dog, because it initiates positive behavior. Your dog hears you say good and he knows that something positive has happened; that he's just completed a desirable thing. It's the first step in getting him to understand what you want from him.

Unfortunately, good can also be used to reinforce negative behavior if you're not careful. Sometimes you'll unconsciously praise your dog with the good word when he's actually involved in undesirable behavior. For example, if you're scratching your dog's back and saying good and the doorbell rings and your dog becomes tense, get your hands off him and stop saying good. Otherwise, you are telling him that becoming tense when the doorbell rings is positive behavior, and it's not. You've got to be on your toes even when you're praising your dog, or else you start reinforcing bad behavior.

No. Contrary to what some people may think, no is a word used to get your dog to clear his head and to start thinking about what you want him to do—it is not a word for punishment. It's a way of "freezing" your dog so commands can be initiated.

To illustrate what's going on when this freeze-state is initiated, consider your dog's ancestor, the wolf, out for a morning stroll in the wild. It's a wonderful day in the meadow: the birds are singing, the sun is shining, the flowers are blooming and Mr. Wolf is feeling pretty optimistic about life.

Who knows what's going on in his head right now? One thing for certain, though, his mind is filled with the clutter of idle noise that surrounds him. It's the same with you although you call it daydreaming or inattentiveness. It's just the way you are, running on auto-pilot half the time because concentrating is work and work is a real pain sometimes. That's what's going on with Mr. Wolf right now. He's not particularly hungry and he has no particular destination in mind, he's just out and about on a pleasant summer morning.

As he goes through the meadow, he passes a bush, a big bush, and suddenly that bush shakes. What does Mr. Wolf do? He freezes. Some people might say something silly like he freezes to become invisible. That is utterly absurd. He's out in the middle of a meadow, and his chances of becoming invisible range from slim to just plain forget it. What's going on during that freeze is that Mr. Wolf is dumping all clutter from his mind and focusing his attention so he can make up his mind about what his options are and which course of action he should take next. His senses are now at work: his nose is twitching to catch a scent, his ears lift to concentrate on sounds, his eyesight focuses, and all his attention is placed on the bush. His body may not be moving, but his brain is anything but frozen right now. This freeze state, then, is a state of high awareness preceding an action.

This is what the word no is supposed to do for your dog when you use it. No conditions your dog to dump all the clutter and focus attention on you. Dogs don't really want to disobey in most cases, but they may develop an undesirable behavior because they can't understand what you want. No is a way of saying, "No, that's not it. I want you to..." It's the stop button to stop a previous behavior so that a new one can be initiated.

The word no is possibly the most misunderstood word you use with your dogs or your kids. You may mistakenly use this word to punish, rather than as a way of getting your dog's attention to give him instructions. As a result, you actually end up teaching negative behavior to the dog. Consider the time when your puppy decides it's time to relieve himself in the house. He starts to squat and you know perfectly well what you're going to do—you're going to turn and roar, "NO! Don't do that!"

All your puppy knows is that he has to relieve himself; he's doing what he thinks he's supposed to be doing, and that's all he's concentrating on at the moment. He's doing something that feels good. Now, somebody is yelling at him. He releases the pleasant clutter in his head, but instead of wondering if it was his squatting on the carpet that you didn't like, he reacts to the volume and body language of your tirade and concludes that flood, fire and famine are on the way; they *must* be, for just look at the way the pack leader is acting.

Not only is he going to run for the hills, he's going to start associating that word no with certain things. A few episodes like this, and he's thinking: "When I hear that word, I had better run for it because something really awful is going to happen." The puppy's owner quickly makes this a truism for the puppy by grabbing him, rubbing the little guy's nose in urine and screeching, "Nononononono. Don't ever do that again!" Any opportunity to educate him has been completely lost because he was never brought into a neutral state of receptiveness in which he would be open to new information. Your puppy has certainly learned a lesson from his ordeal, though not the one you probably thought you were teaching.

No is intended to bring your dog into a receptive state of mind. This means you can't scream, "NOOO! What are you doing? Bad Dog!" when you find your puppy squatting in the middle of the living room. The only thing that's going to condition is a mad flight for safety whenever he hears that word. And, if you grab him, shake him and bring him back to rub his nose in his own urine, do you think you're creating a receptive state of mind in him? Would that work for you?

Both good and no are conditioned vocabulary words. They are words that are used to create a particular state of mind in your dog, establishing either an uncluttered, focused mind that is ready for instruction, or peace of mind through knowing that all is well. These words are the underpinnings of all the command words you use while training your dog.

Concrete Vocabulary

Concrete commands are the easiest ones to teach because they can be physically demonstrated to your dog. It's a good idea to start teaching your dog a series of concrete commands, because not only are you teaching relatively easy commands and working toward more difficult ones, you're also teaching him how to go about learning something in the first place.

When your dog finally discovers that words imply actions, you and your dog can take a simple vocabulary of four to six words and eventually expand it to hundreds. **Once that initial light dawns in your dog that words and actions go together, you have broken through to teaching just about anything.** In addition, some dogs will need more confidence building than others, and helping them learn easy commands in the beginning, with lots of goods accompanying their accomplishments, is a great way to get a dog who feels a bit uncertain about training approach it more enthusiastically.

A typical example of a concrete command is sit. You usually start out teaching puppies this command and several others through food training. You show the puppy a tiny piece of food, so he knows it's in the hand, and then raise it up over his head, saying "sit." In order to raise his head he usually has to lower his rear to look up at you. When he does, you simply say, "Good sit, Bozo." Using this technique also teaches the hand signal for the command, because you're raising your hand up over his head to get him to follow the food into a sitting position, and that's the typical hand signal for that command. He learns to associate both the word and the hand signal with the sitting position all in the same exercise.

Many puppies, and adult dogs, are motivated by food to learn this command. If yours isn't, don't push his rear down in an attempt to get him to sit. That's doing the command for him, and he may never learn to do it himself if he learns he doesn't have to. Instead, put your right hand underneath his collar to steady him, and with your left gently tuck his hind legs under him, saying, "sit." Don't hurt him, just collapse his

Good Sit!

hind legs with your arm just behind his knees, putting him into the sit position, saying, "sit," at the same time. You're demonstrating what you want from him and what that word means. Soon, he should learn that the word sit means to assume a particular position.

Say the word sit just once. If you say it more than once, you're telling him that a response is only necessary after repeated commands. Once he's learned this command, there's no need to repeat yourself. He knows what you want and is making decisions about whether he'll obey. Remember that pack leaders expect and insist on obedience—always. He's got a choice, but you need to show him that it's always much more desirable for him to obey than to disobey.

Concrete commands can be demonstrated to your dog, or your kids for that matter. Anytime you can say Your Dog's Name + Command = Specific Action That Can Be Shown, you're using a concrete command. Because dogs don't use human language, you can use any command word you want to receive the desired response. However, you've got to be consistent about using that chosen command word only for that particular command. This is actually a bit trickier than you might think, and you'll want to give some thought to the command words you choose to accompany a response *before* you start training with them.

Here's an example. You may have heard the ugly rumor that it rains here in Western Washington. Actually, it's no wetter here than in the Amazon Basin, but we get labeled as being a soggy place, anyway. We have patio doors in the kitchen that lead to the back yard, and in front of the doors is a big rug where the dogs have to wait when they come inside to get their feet toweled off. When they come inside, we want them to stop on the rug, but we can't say rug to them, because we already use that word to mean *get on your personal rug*. So, because the rug is in the kitchen, we use the word kitchen to mean they have to stop on the rug, sit, and present their paws for drying. They've learned that kitchen means a specific place and a particular action.

Later, if we're in the kitchen getting dinner going and the dogs come sniffing around for a handout and we want them out of the way, we can't say, "get out of the kitchen," because when they hear that they go to the rug by the patio doors. The phrase "get out of the kitchen" has two of our commands in it: get out and kitchen. Sometimes, we slip when we're concentrating on dinner preparation and say, "get out of the kitchen," before we catch ourselves. Half of the dogs will run to the rug and the other half will get out. Naturally, it's confusing for them. They're *trying* to comply, but we were the ones who got it wrong. Choose your command words carefully, and stick to them. You might want to consider using words that are not only descriptive of the response you want, but are also unlikely to get used inadvertently.

Abstract Commands

An abstract command is one that you can't physically demonstrate to your dog. Consider the word potty or some substitute to start your dog thinking about relieving himself because it's raining and you want him to finish his business fast. The same goes for speak; you can't put your arm down his throat and yank out a bark. Those are abstract words: You can't do them for your dog to show him that's what those words mean. Instead, you condition those words to become commands by associating a command word with your dog's actions whenever he does them. The objective is to observe your dog performing some abstract behavior and then put a word to it so that in time he'll come to associate that word with the particular action. In time, you'll be able to command that action because he has learned that X means such-and-such.

We use the word shake as an abstract command, as opposed to a concrete one like shake hands. We use it to mean shake yourself to shake off water before coming inside or getting in the car. We taught our dogs this command by saying, "good shake," anytime we saw them shaking themselves off, and with Irish Water Spaniels, we had many opportunities to do so. Before long, we were able to command shake and get the desired response. Once that command was conditioned to a response, then using that word for anything else was off limits. When we want a handshake, we have to say, "hello," instead. Be on your toes when choosing your command words. Sometimes you'll find that a word can be descriptive of more than one action, and you'll have to decide which one you want it to apply to, before you start training with it.

Conditioning abstract commands is very satisfying. Because they can't be shown to your dog, it's impressive to watch them doing something on command that appears to be an understanding of abstract concepts on your dog's part. That's always nice for the old ego, too. It's also fun to see your dog comply with an abstract command the first time he's not actively engaged in that particular behavior. You give the command and he looks up at you and you can almost see the wheels turning in his head and the light coming on behind his eyes as he tentatively starts to perform the behavior at your command, rather than just when he felt like it. Dogs just love to know when they're doing the right thing, and when they comply correctly to that first abstract command and get praised for it, they get all excited about learning to do what you wanted.

As a postscript to this description of abstract commands, you should also understand that while it's always possible to condition behavior by associating words or actions with a desired response, it's just as easy to do so unconsciously and teach undesired behavior. In fact, that's just about the most thorough training people do, because they don't realize that they are constantly training their dog every time they interact. Consider how you react to a dog who likes to lick your face. If you've got people in the house who like their dog to do that, and also people in the house who don't, then you're going to need to address the kissing ehavior of your dog.

If you don't, what's going to happen is that the person who doesn't like kisses is going to say, "Stop it! Just knock it off," and push the dog away when licked. Since the dog doesn't realize that it was a specific thing that was unwanted, the only message that's coming through is that he's being totally rejected anytime he gets near that person. "This is awful? The pack leader hates me? What did I do? Guess I better cringe and submit anytime I get near him." Instead, condition your dog to understand that specific action by having the person who likes kisses say, "Good kisses," anytime she gets one.

After she has established that the word kisses goes with a particular action, then that action can be avoided on command. Have a leash on your dog, and after a few slurps, give him a short tug on the leash and say, "No kisses." Now he knows that you're not rejecting *him*, but rather you want a specific behavior to end. It's important to focus on the specific behavior you want to create or negate. You've got to separate it first in your own mind so that you can separate it in your dog's. Otherwise, as in the case of kisses, you're going to be teaching that it's not kisses that you don't like, you don't want to be greeted by your dog at all.

When you train for that specific behavior, then you're saying clearly, "I don't mind you being here, I just don't want my face to feel like it's been through the carwash of love." You might be surprised just how fast your dog can learn that or anything else that you're teaching, whether or not you realize that you *are* teaching him something.

Training Towards Generalization

Corrections

Being pack leader is a big job. You've got to be alert and constantly conscious of your leadership role. Being pack leader is nice, too: you're in charge, looking out for the pack's welfare, and respected for the responsibility that you've taken upon yourself. Being pack leader is a full-time job, with your kids and your dogs. You can't let up, you can't be inconsistent, and you have to maintain your leadership at all times or else that foundation for obedience that you've been working so hard to build starts to crumble like sand under your feet. Being pack leader can be tough, but it's also very rewarding. There's nothing to compare with the satisfaction of having a smoothly running pack in which everyone is comfortable with both themselves and the other pack members. It's a great feeling.

As we said earlier, being a leader means insistence on obedience—always. In a perfect world, everyone would simply do what you wanted them to and everything would be smooth sailing. Most of us have already figured out that it's not a perfect world, at least not all the time, and that means that members of your pack aren't going to do what you want all the time. They've got ideas of their own, after all. As pack leader you know what's best for all concerned, otherwise you wouldn't be pack leader in the first place—they would. So, sometimes members of your pack aren't going to want to do what you know is in their best interests, and as a result you're going to have to pull rank and show them the error of their ways.

With your kids, sometimes you can get this done through discussion, though not always, especially with your very young kids. Two-year-olds just can't grasp the reasons why you want them to do something, so you end up enforcing your wishes. The same is true with your dog. Bozo is often going to be difficult during discussions about why something has to be done the way you want it done, and so you end up enforcing your wishes in some way other than logical discourse.

Having used that word enforced, it's time we talked about what sort of corrections you might use to get your dog to understand that obedience is always preferable to disobedience. First, you need to understand that corrections are not supposed to be a form of physical punishment. You do not need to punish your dog physically. Jerking your dog's head around on a leash for 20 minutes during a training session isn't going to teach him anything, except maybe to get very unhappy when he sees you coming at him with a leash in your hand.

Corrections are intended to notify your dog that an incorrect decision has been made on his part, and that he needs to re-evaluate his response. Corrections are intended to get your dog's attention and to tell him that you insist that he follow your lead. Corrections are accompanied by the word no, for this reason. Like no, they're intended to encourage attention and tell your dog that his response was not what you wanted.

Training collars are one method used for giving corrections. These link-chain collars have taken on the ugly choke-chain label. And, if incorrectly placed on your dog, or incorrectly used, that's what they can do. However, when they're fitted properly and when corrections are correctly performed, they are more appropriately termed check-chains because that's what they're being used to do: check your dog's wandering attention or check an undesired behavior or response. To place the collar on your dog correctly, it is important to decide which side of your body you wish to work him during training.

Traditionally, the dog is on the trainer's left, though you can make up your own mind about what's most comfortable for you. However, assuming that you will in fact be training your dog on your left side, drape a length of the chain through one of the rings so that it forms a loop, with both rings coming together.

Check-chains have two rings, typically referred to as the live ring and the dead ring. The dead ring is so called because it simply lies against the dog's neck, but the live ring is attached to the leash. Place the collar around your dog's head so that the dead ring rests on the side of the neck nearest to you, while the length of chain attached to the live ring runs across the top of the neck towards you

Ultimately, both the live and dead rings will lie atop your dog's neck. You can tell if you've done this properly because the chain will immediately release tension around your dog's neck after corrections. Incorrect placement will not release tension and will choke your dog.

The correction itself is given as a short, quick *pop* with the leash, immediately loosening all tension to the collar afterwards. Don't do this with a regular collar; only use a check-chain because when tension is released from a check-chain, the chain immediately loosens around the dog's neck. A standard collar won't do this, and may injure your dog because unequal pressure is being applied to his neck. With a standard collar, a correction like that would result in jerking his neck.

With a check-chain, the chain quickly tightens with equal pressure all around for a split second, and then releases. Never sustain tension on the leash. That really does create a choke-hold. A short, quick pop with the leash, which then releases the tension immediately afterward, is all you need. Put the check-chain on your forearm and have some-one give you a correction. You'll feel the level of pain involved. Then, compare that to having someone pull on the leash and tug you around—not pleasant at all. Some people will say, "Sure, it doesn't hurt on my arm, but my dog's got it on his neck." Rub your dog's neck with both hands and put your mind at ease. Feel that muscle? His neck is probably a lot more muscular than your arm, even if he's only a small- or medium-sized dog.

Some common sense needs to be involved here. The sort of correction you might apply with a Miniature Pinscher isn't going to be the same you'd use when training a Golden Retriever or a Great Dane. Don't kid yourself, though. Some dogs will require a firmer correction than others. You'll know when you're being too tough or not tough enough. We have many dogs at the Academy who don't even know they're being corrected when a normal or average correction is used: "Huh? What was that?" Sometimes, we don't even get that much response from some breeds. Use some common sense and you'll discover what's appropriate.

As with most other aspects of training, the particular dog you're working with and the circumstances under which you're working him will to some extent determine the appropriate level of correction to use. With a puppy it's a mistake to be too tough on him. Not only has his training just begun, but he's also just a little guy. If you're too firm with him at such a young age, you're likely going to end up with a mechanical obedience from him, caused by pain or fear.

On the other hand, if you're working with a relatively dominant dog who wants to challenge your leadership at every turn, you're going to have to impress on him that you're the pack leader and that you insist on being obeyed. For the most part, it's this later instance in which people fail to match the correction to the need. With a little puppy you seem to know that it's best to be firm but to not overdo it.

Unfortunately, you may fail to give an older dog the appropriate level of correction because, well, you love him and may think that you're being too tough on him. This often happens when you get a dog as a puppy and he grows up with you. It's sometimes hard to think that in just 22 to 24 weeks he's not a puppy anymore, but a full-blown teenager with lots on his mind to distract him. You may still gush over everything he does, and find it hard to be firm with him, even when he's demonstrating the need for it.

While we're on the subject of corrections, it's worth noting that there are a few other types of corrections that can be used in certain situations to help end undesirable behavior in your dog. In many cases, you will find that it's nearly impossible to correct a certain behavior because your dog doesn't engage in it while you've got a leash on him, so you can't administer a leash correction.

You know the feeling when you hear funny noises coming from under the hood of the car and as soon as you take it to the mechanic it won't make the noise, and as soon as you get home it starts acting up again. If you've got a dog who likes to bark through the fence at the neighbor's dog and you stick your head out the window and yell, "Quiet," and he keeps on barking, your first response is to go and get the check-chain and the leash and walk him up and down the fence until he barks again so you can correct him for it. But, once that leash is on you discover that your dog has suddenly become mute. You say, "Good quiet, Bozo," and go back inside. Five minutes later he's doing his Placido Domingo rendition for the dog next door again. You rush out and put the leash back on, and your dog immediately acts as if he's in a library. At times like this, conventional training exercises won't allow you to correct this behavior. Something else is needed.

Noisemakers of various kinds often work wonders with this kind of behavior problem. Try putting some pennies and pebbles in an old pop can and tape the lid shut. When your dog starts telling off the neighbor's dog, sling that can out the window and against the fence if you can manage it. Try not to be seen by your dog when you throw the can. The idea is to get the dog to associate the startling noise of the banging can with his barking at the fence. Once that can hits the ground, your dog will usually stop barking, if not for good, then at least for awhile. That's when you stick your head out the window and say, "Good quiet, Bozo." Sudden sounds will often catch your dog's attention. The idea isn't to frighten him, but rather to get his attention diverted from his previous behavior so that you can reinforce another one. It's a way of breaking through distractions so you can instruct him.

Corrections of this kind can be performed when you're not around. To break a dog from getting on a counter, a stack of empty pop cans on a cookie sheet that is precariously perched on the brink of the counter will make a wonderful racket when your dog yields to the temptation of a tasty morsel left for him up there. You need to stifle your snickers from the other room when this is going on, however.

We did this once with a dog who was a notorious forager. He would stand on his hind legs and put his snout up on the counter for reconnaissance. He was often rewarded with something that was inadvertently left there during the night, so he was actually being trained that such sneaky behavior was worthwhile. I happened to be nearby during a training session with him when he tipped the tray. I could have sworn he said, "Run for it," when that tray hit the floor. His parents later remarked that, after a few more tries with this, they never had a problem with his counter-sweeping again.

While this is an effective means of correcting this type of unwanted behavior, never do it with a dog going through a fear imprint stage. No reason to have your dog start acting weird whenever you pull a can of pop out of the refrigerator.

Sometimes even things like cold squirts of water from a squirt bottle can be effective in ending unwanted behavior. A baying Beagle who would just as soon serenade you until sunrise may find a squirt or two of cold water on the snout not conducive to yodeling.

If your dog doesn't particularly mind a spritz of seltzer, try adding a bit of vinegar to the water. In either case, the idea isn't to drown your dog with the squirt bottle, but rather to startle him, so that you break through his current behavior and insert instructions to countermand what he's doing. If you're good enough to be sneaky, a squirt out of nowhere is the best. Then comes the, "No, stop that," that will inform him that the pack leader isn't much interested in his singing career.

We've had clients who had dogs that exhibited the alarming propensity for chewing plugged-in electrical cords. That's behavior that needs to be shorted-out in a hurry. A liberal application of hot pepper oil on all their electrical cords was a sure-fire way of ending a shocking taste in chew toys.

Other types of startling corrections can be used, given the situation and what you've got on hand. Keep in mind that the idea is to startle, never harm or instill genuine fear. We once told a client that mousetraps might work to keep his dog off the couch while he was gone, but before we could explain, he looked as if he thought he'd walked into the Northwest Center for Sadism. We went on to explain that the loaded traps are placed under a single sheet of newspaper so that they just make a loud pop, not pinching the dog when he jumps up to occupy the pack leader's turf in his absence. He seemed relieved after our explanation. We were too.

Corrections, no matter what form they take, are intended to break through distractions and create a state of mind in your dog that is receptive to instruction. It's important to understand that your dog can become *very* distracted at times.

For example, when another dog comes running up and all you seem to be able to do is pull back on his leash, you need a way of breaking through to get your instructions out to him. Corrections are necessary. Without them, you will find it difficult, if not impossible, to insist on obedience and demonstrate that, as pack leader, you demand obedience always.

A good correction must meet the following standards:

> It must not be made while you are angry or emotional or you stand a very good chance of the dog focusing on your

emotions and totally missing the message you are trying to send.

It must be made quickly and with as much "startle" as possible. Prolonged corrections quickly become punishment.

It must allow your dog to come away from the correction free from fear. A correction should not terrify your dog.

TRAINING AND GENERALIZING

Earlier, we talked about the way to create obedience through leadership, consistency and generalizing training. On the face of it, this sounds straight-forward: you establish your leadership, you remain consistent in following the rules, and you insist on obedience in every situation. As you saw earlier, establishing and maintaining your leadership isn't always easy, what with all the things that go on in life.

Nor is it always convenient to be consistent, because it's hard to stay on your toes all the time, and everybody wants to take time off now and then. Sometimes it's hard work being pack leader.

Luckily, that notion of generalization sounds easy enough: you just keep training your dog, or your kids, in any kind of situation, and in the end you've demonstrated that obedience is a constant thing; the rules always apply. Not bad. Well, we hate to break it to you, but there can be some complications with that part of the process, too. Let's talk about how the training really proceeds, and you'll see how it works and see some of the hurdles that need to get jumped along the way.

Let's return to the simplest command of all—sit. Earlier you saw that training the sit is one of the easiest commands to teach because, for one, it's a concrete command and can be demonstrated to your dog, and for another it comes naturally to your dog because he needs to sit to be able to look up at you.

Thank goodness for easy commands to teach. Then, in order to generalize this command you simply work on sit all over the place, wherever and whenever you can, increasing the level of distraction as you go. Simple enough. He knows the command response now, so all you need to do is just insist that he sit no matter where you are or what's going on. No problem. Now, ask your dog to sit while he's lying down. Ah ha? He looks at you and says: "My butt is on the ground. What's your problem? Why are you shaking your head like that?"

You may be thinking that he's trying to pull something on you, perhaps challenging your leadership, but he doesn't really know what you want. Too bad you can't ask: "By the way, Bozo, just what *does* sit mean to you?" and get an answer. If you could, you might learn that, to him, it means to put his rump on the ground and look up. Well, when he's laying down, that's just what he's doing. And, after all, that's what he's learned so far when you've been doing sits before. He's standing, he hears the sit command, and the rump goes to the floor and he looks up at you. Now it's different.

In this instance, sit isn't a verb, it's a noun; it's not an action, it's a place, a position. You need to demonstrate that important difference to him. You can do this the same way you taught him to sit in the first place: by showing him. But, generalization hasn't been achieved yet, even though you've got him to sit from a down position. Next, stand behind a wall where you can still see your dog but he can't see you, and ask him to sit. Does he? There's a pretty good chance he won't. Why?

Coming back to the way dogs see and understand us, and how they go about learning from us, consider the fact that while you've been teaching and later commanding him to sit all this time, quite a bit has been going on besides his hearing that word sit and his eventual response to it. Quite likely your dog has been learning sit from you by means other than the command word alone.

As we discussed earlier, dogs are incredibly sensitive to body language, and even if you haven't been using a hand signal all the time to accompany your command, chances are that your body language was telling him to sit when you gave that command. Whether or not you realized, you were likely snapping your fingers or raising your eyebrows or standing up really straight or using some nonverbal cue when you were teaching that command.

Now that your body is hidden behind a wall, to your dog, sit only means sit if certain other things, such as body language, accompany that word. To achieve true generalization you need to train your dog to understand that sit must be obeyed as a verbal command alone, and that he cannot rely on accompanying gestures or other nonverbal cues to understand your intentions.

Good so far? Well, there's more. One of the trickiest things to get your dogs to understand is your human sense of focus, particularly regarding the elapsing of time. How long will your dog sit for you? Until you turn away? Maybe for a minute or so? That's not bad, but if you intend to insist on obedience in any situation, your dog will need to learn that command responses must be maintained until he is released from them. If your dog doesn't remain sitting when someone comes through the door, it means that you haven't educated him to the point where he understands that sit *still* means sit, despite distractions.

Since we're on the subject of time, you should be aware that there's a big difference between asking your dog to maintain a command and asking him to do something over and over and over as part of a training exercise. No matter how well-trained or how eager to please you your dog is, no dog is going to give you unlimited repetitions to a command.

It's just not going to happen. Let's say we're out with Deuce, our best-trained dog, and we're walking her around outside and every so often we say sit. We keep doing this, over and over again: sit/walk/sit. At some point Deuce is finally going to turn around as if to say, "What's going on here, anyway? Why am I doing all these sits? You think I'm some kind of moron, or what? We'll see about that." Very soon, we're going to lose Deuce's sit.

Even though we could get the sit back by praising her when she did so, or correcting her when she didn't, no matter how you look at it, that kind of repetitiveness isn't constructive. Deuce will go a long time before asking why because we have a good relationship. In the end, though, we'd be jeopardizing that relationship by driving that command into the ground when it wasn't necessary.

If you've got a dog that's new to the learning process, it won't take many repetitions before he says, "Excuse me, we've already done this a couple of times. What's going on?" Respect your dog's boredom and his level of patience. Respect is a two-way street after all. Imagine helping your kids learn to spell by using flashcards. After a while, they're going to start saying, "Stop it. I already know how to spell Australopithecus." Your own patience may be unfathomable, but your kid's or your dog's may stop far short of yours.

Generalization can be accomplished although it may be more complicated than just saying the command in different environments. Don't get discouraged if it takes you longer than you think to get there with a particular command. It'll happen. Without achieving generalization, you'll end up like the woman with the ring-smart dog: you'll have obedience under some conditions, but never true control. That means you find yourself without the ability to control him when you most want to, like when he dashes out into traffic or takes off howling at the new neighbors.

The same will be true with your children. Getting them to eat their vegetables happily might be nice, but when they dash out into traffic you'll want to be able to exert immediate control and be obeyed instantly. Generalization, built on the foundation of leadership and consistency, needs to be applied to both your dogs and your kids, or the obedience you want just won't be there when you really need it.

DROP OR DOWN

Drop or down, like so many other of the commands recommended by the American Kennel Club, had a solid reason behind it when first introduced as part of competition obedience training. The original intent of the command was designed for times when working or companion dogs encountered a stream or some other hazard. The owner could then drop the dog into a prone position wherever he was and then, after determining that potential dangers had passed, release the dog to follow. This is still a very useful command, even if you're not out in the field dodging rapids or similar hazards.

One benefit of teaching this command is that it allows the dog to maintain a stable position for longer periods of time than does a sit. A sit can become uncomfortable after awhile for your dog, and his natural inclination is to lie down if stationary for more than a minute or so. If you greet a friend on the street and become involved in a lengthy conversation, it's better to have your dog in a down than a sit because it's more comfortable for him.

A down can be a good way to get your dog to cool off after some exciting play. Lying down is relaxing and calming. And, yes, there are times when you might need to have your dog down by the stream so that you can cross over the footbridge first without having to do your tightrope act as he dashes past you to the other side: "C'mon. That old cedar log is plenty wide enough to run across." Well, maybe for four feet, but with your handicap it's nice to have your dog lying down until you can get across first.

Training the down towards generalization will require you to start out using a leash and getting him to down relatively nearby. As his learning progresses, the length of that leash can increase. Ultimately, you want to be able to down him even if he's running toward or away from you. You may find a long line helpful for working him during that stage. And, like other commands to be generalized, you will need to work with him in a variety of settings and situations.

Part of the generalization process requires you to train using different voice inflections. This is particularly true of commands like drop, come and leave it, because those are the ones you most often employ in stressful situations and your voice is going to be considerably different from the voice you use while doing training in the back yard.

Many people who are interested in obedience training end up training for the competition ring and neglect to generalize their commands. As a result, they have no control over their dogs in the real world, and this often shows up in the way they try to demand obedience under the pressures of real-world problems. Their dogs start heading for traffic and they get all flustered. It's no longer the ring in which disobedience results in losing points; this time it's serious. They either forget the command word, or else they're screaming, "DOWN," in such an unfamiliar way that the dogs havn't the slightest idea what they're saying. All they're hearing is the fear in their voices, and if the pack leaders are scared of something, they're thinking they'd be idiots not to be scared, too. Likely, they just bolt because they are not used to being addressed like that. Generalize your commands with vocal variations.

It doesn't really matter if you use the word drop or the word down when teaching this command. For that matter, you could say "Zulu bangles" if you wanted to, as long as you remained consistent about what that meant.

Some people like to use the word drop because they associate down with other things. For example, if your dog is up on the couch and you tell him down and that's your command word for lying down, that's just what he'll do—stretch himself out on the couch. If that's what you had in mind, fine. But if you intended to get him off the couch, down isn't the word for it.

This command is not intended to tell the dog to change his elevation, but rather to assume the prone position. Sometimes you instinctively say the word down when that's not what you intended, because that's the way you use that word. If your dog jumps up on somebody and you say, "down," and he lowers his front legs and gets rewarded for it, because that was what you were hoping he'd do, then you've just confused him. Get yourself clear on your commands and stick to them. None of this sit-down, lie-down, get-down stuff. That's too confusing for your dog.

Down is also used to signal your dog that you are pack leader. Putting your dog in a down position is sending the message that you are superior—above—to your dog. Again, height is might, and pack leaders always take the high ground. If he's reluctant to do a down, there's a good chance that he's telling you that he's not going to accept your authority. At that point, it's time to insist on obedience and use your corrections.

In some cases, it may not be a challenge to your leadership that makes a dog reluctant to down for you. If someone or some animal walks into the room unexpectedly, many dogs will want to be on their feet in case it's a fight-or-flight situation they're confronting. Being down is a vulnerable position. However, by teaching your dog to be in a down in hectic situations, you can build his confidence in understanding that he can handle those situations after all. After maintaining the down for awhile, he can see that nothing's happened to him. If a fearful or insecure dog is allowed to run and hide behind the couch every time there's a new encounter, he'll never master his fear. When socializing your dog to new situations, having him do a down can be handy.

STAY AND DOWN-STAY

The most important thing your dog needs to learn about stay is the binding nature of this command. Stay is an absolute. That is, when you put your dog in a stay, he must remain in that place and in that position, despite any distractions, until he is physically released by you. He cannot move until you walk over to him, touch him and say, "Okay." When training, if he moves from his position, walk over to him, take his leash and correct him, adding the word no to indicate that he made the wrong choice, and then replace him with the word stay in the same place he was prior to moving.

Generalizing this command is an exercise in demonstrating your insistence on obedience and is also an effective means of strengthening your dog's attention span. He learns that he must stay in any setting and under any set of circumstances, and at the same time he learns to maintain his focus on obedience for longer periods of time. Teaching stay can be one of the trickiest commands of all to teach because it requires your dog to remain focused on what he's doing for longer than is normal for him.

His notion of time is much different from yours and, for him, being obedient to a command may be understood as only a temporary situation: "There, that oughta be long enough. I got that stay down pretty good if I do say so myself. Now I'll just mosey on over and see about that bone over there and...Whoa? What's she so ticked off about?" It will be necessary to create an increasingly demanding series of exercises to aid in generalizing this command.

Continuing to generalize this command will also require you to step up the level of distractions your dog faces while he's doing a stay. Has he got a favorite toy, or does he go bonkers when there's even a hint of getting something to eat? If so, those are your tools for distraction. Toss that ball past him, or sprinkle those treats just out of his reach. Don't worry, it's not torture. He can have them as a reward later on for successfully maintaining his stay.

Other things to be taught while working toward generalization with this command involve your proximity to your dog when giving the command and when the command is being obeyed. Work on giving this command while you're some distance away from your dog. If he complies, then it's a good stay, Bozo. After that, try walking away out of his line of sight, but where you can still see him. If he moves, go back to him and correct and replace him. He'll need to learn that you insist on obedience even if you're out of sight. This is the same thing with your kids, too.

You can't expect obedience at home and then send them off to school and let them run amok. When they come home with one of those letters from the teacher, you've got to teach that obedience is insisted upon always, not just when you're there watching them.

Both stay and wait are indicators to your dog of your status as pack leader. Wait allows you to go through doors first, or to get to a certain place first. Leaders always go first. If you've got several dogs at home, watch how they figure out who goes through the door first. This is a big deal for dogs, and so it should be with you, too, if you're interested in establishing and maintaining your leadership.

The down-stay is a type of the stay to allow keeping your dog comfortable while complying with your command that he stay. To sit on a lengthy stay gets tiresome for your dog and may erode his ability to comply willingly with your wishes. Remember, stay means not only to maintain a particular place, it also means that he has to maintain a particular position. If he's put into a stay while he's sitting, that means he can't lie down. After a while, it's going to get harder and harder for him to obey, and that's not what you want. There's no point in setting up your dog for failure. That would be like the boss handing you a project that was sure to fail, just so she could watch you squirm a bit. No need for that sort of thing.

A down-stay is handy while you're eating dinner or there's lots of excitement around you and you want your dog to be out of the way, but still comfortable. If you have guests drop in who really aren't dog-loving people, it's nice to have your dog on a long down-stay until they leave. Don't worry about him lying around for hours at a time. Dogs do it all the time. So do you, for that matter.

Leave It

Leave it is the command most representative of the benefits and applications of generalization in training. Because it is so versatile and can be used in so many settings and situations, leave it is just about everyone's favorite command. Leave it is the next best thing to being able to say, "Stop it," whenever your dog is engaged in some unwanted behavior. It's probably even better than stop it because with leave it you don't even have to wait for your dog to become fully engaged in unwanted behavior before you negate it. Isn't that great? If you can successfully generalize this command, you will have a very powerful tool for obedience always at the ready for just about any situation.

The leave it command means that your dog must not only leave something alone—like disengage from chewing on something—but he must turn his attention away from it, physically if that's what it takes to ensure that he's no longer considering starting up again. This command can be applied even when you've just got suspicions that some unwanted behavior *might* take place.

When you're at the park with your dog, he's not hurting anything by just looking at another dog. But, if he starts to get that gleam in his eyes that says, "I'd just love to chomp on that arrogant so-and-so over there," you've got a good clue that he's *about to* initiate some unwanted behavior. So, it's a "No, Bozo. Leave it." If he does what he's been taught to do, turn away from what he had been focusing on, then it's a, "Good leave it, Bozo." You have effectively maintained obedience before any actual disobedience was evident.

If you accidentally drop a tasty morsel of chicken on the floor, you've got to be quick if you hope to use leave it effectively. You have to say that command as fast as lightning and have it be obeyed.

People who have dogs rarely have to worry about what to do with food that inadvertently falls on the floor. In moments, your little *Hoover*-with-a-tail is there to clean up the mess. The problem with dropped food is that if your dog is gobbling the chicken while you're saying leave it, he's getting rewarded for disobeying the command. If he does obey you, you need to reward him in some other fashion, praise or maybe a handy doggy treat. He went through a fair bit of agony to leave that chicken alone, so he should be recompensed for his trouble.

Leave it eliminates the need to come up with hundreds of specific commands to accommodate potential unwanted behaviors. Besides, you'll have a hard time anticipating all the trouble your dog can get into. How can you know in advance that one day your dog will take a liking for chewing on your child's toys? Or that, after all these years of peaceful coexistence, he suddenly takes a strong dislike to the cat? Leave it eliminates the need for foresight.

When your dog understands leave it, you can sit your partially finished plate on the coffee table, say leave it, and exit the room. Your dog knows he's not supposed to go over and sniff it, sample it or touch it in any way because it's yours and nobody else's. We have a paper maché reindeer by the fireplace that never ceases to attract the keen interest of our dogs. When we tell our dogs to leave it, we expect them to not only leave it alone, but also to look away and to divert their attention to something else. When they do, we say, "Good leave it," and give some physical praise, because they should be rewarded for obeying.

This physical praise can also help ensure that their attention is diverted from whatever it was that you wanted them to leave alone. That's important. If they haven't really diverted their attention, then the *good* part of good leave it is praising them for disobedience.

For example, your dog is lying down and your cat comes strolling along. Your dog raises up on his haunches in preparation to savage the cat. You say, "Bozo, leave it." When Bozo sinks back down, you say, "Good Bozo," right? Wrong. Bozo is still looking at the cat, thinking: "Kill the cat. I must kill the cat. Cats are evil. Kill, kill, kill." And, while this little mantra is playing through his head, you're saying, "Good, Bozo." Instead, Bozo has to more than physically relax, he has to actually turn his attention toward something else. If he turns to you to get petted, his attention has been successfully redirected.

How do you tell a child to leave it? Do you wail and gnash your teeth for your child as a way of informing him that you really, *really* want him to leave something alone, or do you redirect his two-year-old attention by substituting some other distraction? If you see parents at the grocery store with their small children and notice they've got a key chain that looks like it's a tangle of plastic ornaments and doo-dads, then you know how they go about getting leave it to work with their kids. "No, leave the sugar-coated cherry whompers alone. No, don't grab the gummy-slugs, either. Where's your sister? In the bulk foods? Here, don't touch anything and play with this neat-o key chain while I find her." Teaching leave it includes finding something else to do, and that goes for all your kids.

Keep in mind that your little kids and your dog may understand leave it in a rather temporary way until you've thoroughly generalized it. Like the little girl with the expensive vase, she may have a hard time at first understanding that leave it means for more than just a minute or two. It's going to take a bit of repetition and reinforcement until she understands, "Oh. You mean don't touch it *ever*?" The same is true with your dogs. Remember when we talked about teaching your puppy to sit, and he did just fine in the kitchen, but two minutes later out in the living room he couldn't understand what you were asking him to do? Same thing with leave it. It's going to take a while until he understands: "Oh. You mean I have to leave it alone over *here*, too?" In time, you can get leave it generalized to the point where you can divert your dog's attention away from any unwanted behavior.

Come or Come Here

While leave it is usually most people's favorite command, come is right up there in the rankings. You want to be able to call your dog and have him come running to you. It's a great feeling to be out in a big field with your dog way out ahead of you and then shout, "Come," and watch him come tearing back to the ol' pack leader.

The flip-side is that it's incredibly embarrassing to be out in the park, screaming, "Bozo, come," and have your dog utterly ignore you. Whenever that happens, you probably take off running after their dog, only to learn quickly that four legs can move a lot faster than two. Bozo is having a great time watching you running after him. It's a great game for him, particularly because the top dog always leads the game. "Hey, he's chasing *me*? Allllright." More than just being embarrassing, Bozo's lack of response to come might cost him his life someday if he ignores you when a truck is bearing down on him. Teaching your dog to come on command is probably one of the most important commands he can learn.

It's also the command that most people have trained their dogs not to do. You do this because you punish your dogs when they finally do come back to you after having made you scream come at them all over the park. If you're like most people, in the early going of your training you find that your dog won't always come on command when you're out doing something your dog finds interesting. He wants to run over here and sniff that thing over there, and he wants to have fun. All this time, though, you've been screaming: "Bozo, come. Bozo, you come right now or I'll..."

And sure enough, that's what you do. Either you finally catch your dog or else he finally figures: "Oh, all right. Keep your pants on, I'm coming." Then, when you get hold of him you're yelling and gesturing and making it real plain to him that staying away was really in his best interests after all. "Just see if I come next time, pal," is what he's think-ing. In a matter of just one outing you've managed to connect some-thing negative to the action of coming to you, and now the word come is a signal for punishment. Would *you* run over to someone who was threatening you?

Training should be a positive experience, for both you and your dog. Most often, when it's pleasant for him, it ends up being pleasant for you because he's happily doing what you want him to do. If you've got a puppy, start him on that positive training experience right from the start by teaching him come.

You can teach a puppy to come through what's referred to as Re-verse Chaining. This is a momentary restraint of the puppy who is then released to do what he wanted to do all along: come back to you. When we're doing a Puppy Private at the Academy, we'll get down on the floor with a puppy and start playing with him, rubbing his belly and trying to make him feel good. We'll be saying, "Good come," to him, even if he's just squirming around on our laps.

We want him to know, right from the start, that come is a good word. Next, we'll pick him up and set him about six inches away, holding him back just a little. He loves all the attention he's been getting, so when we let him go he dives right back onto our laps for some more. This is when we say, "Good come. That was a really good come, wasn't it?" And, he's getting absolutely smothered with affection now. Then we pick him up and set him back 12 inches. Sure enough, as soon as we release him he can't wait to get back for some more belly rubs. Then we coo at him: "Ohhh, that was a wonderful come. You're so special. That was a really good come." What's happening is that the little guy is getting his first introduction to that word, and boy does it feel good. As time goes by, if you are consistent about the positive nature of that word, you can have him come anytime.

Most people don't realize what they're teaching a little puppy half the time. If the little guy runs up and gives you a slurp on the face and you respond with an, "Ugh? Get away," and you push him off. That's utter rejection as far as he's concerned. He doesn't know that it was specifically the slurp you didn't like. All he knows is that you don't really want him coming up to you. Chances are, next time he won't and you'll be stumped by his reluctance.

As with so many other commands, generalizing come will require you to use vocal variations so you can be understood by your dog even during times of stress. If he only understands that word when it's spoken in a certain way and with a certain gesture or posture to accompany it, chances are he won't respond favorably when the truck is headed his way and you're screaming, "Bozo! COME," with all your might. More likely, he'll just bolt off blindly because the pack leader is in a state of high agitation and that means that something bad is going to happen. "The pack leader is frantic about something? Don't know what it is, but I'm not gonna stick around to find out. I'm outta here."

People often fall down on their training this command, and others, because they confuse the word with other commands. You wouldn't believe how many folks we've watched in obedience training classes telling their dogs to sit down. Now, which one is it, anyway, sit or down? Same thing happens with the come command. "Come on, hurry and go outside. Come on, eat your dinner. Come on, go to your rug."

What's the deal? Do you want your dog to come or go? Get your vocabulary straight in your own mind, and be consistent.

Failure to come on your dog's part just might be a signal that your leadership is not all that it should be. If that's the case, you'd better start working on your leadership skills because trying to get your dog to do anything is going to be a struggle. On the other hand, failure to come might be the result of other influences. Sometimes it's a matter of the breed you're working with.

For example, a Beagle is bred to get on the track of something and leave his leader in order to follow the trail. A Beagle may do that because he instinctively believes that there's a reward for him at the end. However, for the average dog, it is not natural for him to want to run away from his leader. In other cases, if your dog is leaving you and hoofing it down the street, it's possible that he's being rewarded for that behavior.

Maybe the dog down the street is a lot more fun to play with than you are, or maybe he's heading for his favorite garbage can that never fails to produce an interesting tidbit or two. Your own rewards for come are going to have to counteract that. He may only come for the highest bidder.

As a postscript to this discussion of training your commands towards generalization, you should never set yourself up for failure when training, no matter what you're trying to train. Don't put yourself in situations in which your training is most likely to fail.

For example, you get up to go get something from the other room and you turn to your dog and say, "stay." As you leave the room, you turn and there he is, right at your side following you around. You're in a hurry to get that thing from the other room and you don't have the time or patience to take him back in the other room and put him back in his stay. You just failed in your training.

You're lying in bed at night and your dog is thrashing around and keeping you awake. "Bozo, down." However, Bozo just wanders off to the living room and eventually settles down out there. You're too tired to get up and correct him, and besides he's being quiet now and that's all you wanted. You just failed again. If you're going to give a command, you'd better be prepared to enforce it. If you aren't, then you're being inconsistent and your dog learns that you don't always have to be obeyed. There's no chance for generalization of your commands if you're teaching him that he doesn't always have to obey. Don't set yourself up for failure. Set aside uncluttered time to train, and the rest of the time be consistent. If you can't enforce obedience to a command, don't ask.

Training toward generalization is exceptionally satisfying. When just a handful of commands have become generalized, you can be happy with your dog because you can expect obedience always. That's what being leader is all about. It's also what you most want out of parenting. You want to be able to expect obedient and appropriate behavior from your dogs and your kids every time and in any situation. After all, you *are* the parents, and that puts you in charge and obligates you to look out for the welfare of the whole pack. Luckily, most of you have a good sense of what's in the best interests of the whole pack, so you should want to have your pack members follow your lead. With that attitude, and with generalized obedience, you can expect to have a happy pack at home—or anywhere.

HOUSETRAINING

You're never going to be thoroughly happy until you teach that little ball of fuzz that the toilet is over *there*. There's nothing like making a midnight raid on the fridge, successfully overcoming the obstacle of building a satisfying sandwich in the dark, and then, on your way to the table, stepping in a little surprise left behind by the newest addition to the family. For some reason, you just lost your appetite. Looks like it's time to start getting serious with the housetraining.

Basic housetraining means establishing an allowable toilet area for puppies, or older dogs, who are new to your home. If your dog is relieving himself in the house simply because he doesn't know where else he can do so when he needs to, then he falls into this category.

Submissive wetting, however, is not about your dog's lack of understanding of where he can and can't relieve himself. This behavior relates exclusively to urinating in the house and generally coincides with what your dog sees as a stressful situation requiring some sort of submissive response on his part. It may occur during greetings, disciplining, or in other situations in which your dog gets excited about something. If a puddle appears after the doorbell rings, don't start looking at the ceiling for leaks. Likely, it's your dog literally giving vent to his stress about strangers coming through the door.

Marking is something altogether different. Both male and female dogs exhibit this behavior, but it's only seen in dogs that have reached puberty. Marking can include both defecation and urine, but usually a dog will urinate somewhere as a means of pointing out his territory. Dogs will mark territory like this even when all necessary urination is finished. Your dog will dash from place to place, lift his leg and deposit a drop or two here and there, basically saying: "This is mine...and this is mine...and this is mine." If your dog is older than four months and appears to have a problem with either submissive wetting or marking, get professional advice. These things are behavior related, and it's not always going to be clear to you what's causing this behavior to surface. You might be surprised. Get some help.

For one thing, using your house as a toilet area might actually be beyond your dog's ability to control. Make sure there are no medical problems that can complicate the issue. Urinary tract infections or an intestinal upset are relatively common, and they can make your attempts at housetraining difficult. Some medications can interfere with your housetraining. In addition, some foods have a laxative-like effect on your dog. That can make it difficult to try to housetrain your dog. Can you imagine being locked in a room all day after gobbling down a handful of laxatives? You might find your own housetraining a bit hard to maintain in a situation like that.

If you're committed to housetraining and prepared for it from the first moment you introduce your new puppy or dog to your home, basic housetraining should take you about two weeks. This is a relatively small price to pay for a lifetime of stain- and odor-free carpets. On the other hand, if your new addition to the family has already developed bad habits about relieving himself, you should expect to take closer to six weeks or more to establish reliable housetraining behavior. In either case, you need to be prepared to invest the necessary time and energy if you want positive results. Anything less is going to cost you more down the line.

What is an appropriate toilet area for your dog? That's up to you. It can be as general as outside, or it can be as specific as a litterbox, depending on your preferences and your situation. Wherever it is, though, you've got to be clear in your own mind what that place will be before you start training your dog. Your dog can be trained to use a specific corner of the yard, for example, if you're willing to put in the necessary effort required to train him to that finite degree of understanding.

Your attitude when housetraining your dog is the most important part of creating an effective formula for getting your dog to understand where he's supposed to go when he needs to. Remember, this is going to be a process of very basic education. He has no idea whatsoever that you consider it wrong for him to use your living room as a toilet: His mother never told him about that, and neither was this knowledge genetically pre-programmed into him at birth. If anything, your dog is likely to view your carpet as a *perfect* place to relieve himself. Consider its wonderful features: It's soft so there's no nasty splashing; it's absorbent so things just magically disappear into it; and, best of all, it's readily available. What could be better? As a result, it's your job to help him figure out that he has to relieve himself where you want him to.

ESCORT YOUR DOG TO THE TOILET AREA

Take your dog to the place you've decided is his future toilet and stand by quietly while he investigates the area. This is not play time. Don't distract him with overtures to play or by saying hurry up or go potty or whatever else you intend to use later on as a command to get him to relieve himself. Just let him investigate for awhile. About three to five minutes is long enough for this part of the training. If he doesn't relieve himself during that time, take him back in the house and contain him for half an hour, either in a doggy-crate or in a tiled room that you've cordoned off with a gate of some sort, and then try it again. You might want to set a timer for this in case you forget.

Eventually, you're going to coincide with his natural desire to go. When you're with him in the toilet area and he finally does start to go, quietly and calmly praise him while he's doing so. Use good plus the word or phrase that you've selected for this particular response: good potty or good hurry up, or whatever it is you want to use. You've escorted him out to begin to associate that word with this action.

Remember, he can't learn an abstract command like this any other way. When he's done, then praise him with more enthusiasm. You want that word associated with that action, and you want that word to be a good thing for him.

Start to learn your dog's habits. Some dogs need to urinate two or three times at an outing to be satisfied. This is often followed by a bowel movement. In addition, if the weather is bad and you're reluctant to take your dog out to relieve himself, don't let your dog sense this. They can pick up on your emotions very easily. If that happens, you may inadvertently create a dog who is reluctant to go outside to relieve himself during nasty weather.

Part of learning his habits involves using common sense about when he's most likely to want to relieve himself. Take him out when he wakes up, after he eats, and after all your play sessions.

CREATE A SCHEDULE FOR YOUR DOG

What's going on during this time is that you're creating a schedule for him to use the toilet area. Make one that's convenient for both of you, but the emphasis should be on making it convenient for you. This schedule includes meal times. Serve them on a regular basis. Don't allow your dog to eat whenever he wants during the time you're setting up a housetraining schedule. Snacks and treats should be kept to a minimum during this time, and you should avoid giving him any rich foods that might upset his bowels.

As a part of setting up this schedule, establish specific times for your dog to go to bed and to wake up. Try to stick to these as closely as you can. Like all youngsters, a puppy is going to need lots of naps between full-fledged sleeps. Make sure your schedule allows for them. Whenever he wakes up, take him to the established toilet area.

You're going to need to keep an eye on his other activities as well. Any time a dog has been emotionally stimulated, like having been badly frightened by the cat or having participated in some rowdy playtime, he's going to feel the call. Take him to the toilet area again. Most dogs will be able to exercise self-restraint for the eight hours during the night after only two or three days of keeping on a schedule, but daytime schedules involve more variables. Because of that, you're going to have to supervise and educate your dog, and you'll need to establish a daytime schedule that you both can live with.

SUPERVISE IN THE HOUSE:

If you know where your dog is at all times, you can observe him and catch him before he makes a mistake. If he begins to relieve himself where he's not supposed to, firmly, but calmly, say, "No," and immediately take him to the proper place for his business. Don't yell at him or chase him around. If you're home but don't feel like you can constantly supervise him, tie his leash to a doorknob in the area where you are. If you're going to sit down and read or watch TV for awhile, use a leash or long-line while you're doing so. That way, he can't wander off to another room and make a mistake. Before you settle in, give him some toys to play with. Nobody, canine or human, likes to be bored.

If you work for a living, you're not going to be able to keep an eye on him all the time. During those times, he's going to need to be contained somewhere, either in a place that he's unwilling to use as a toilet, like his dog crate, or in a place where accidents can be accepted. Places with tiled floors are usually the best choice, provided that things like wastepaper baskets, towels or other intriguing items are beyond his reach. If you're not crazy about the possibility of him having an accident in the house while you're away, try fencing off a corner of your garage. Don't leave him with food and water if you're only going to be away a few hours, and don't load him up on treats before you go. How would you like to be told to hold it all day after you just loaded up your stomach and bladder with a big breakfast and a pot of coffee?

If you're going to be gone longer than eight hours, you'll need to get a friend or neighbor to drop by and give your dog something to drink and a chance to relieve himself. That's just common courtesy for another living creature.

Caught in the Act

If you ever catch your dog relieving himself in the house, quietly but firmly say, "No." If you feel the need to add volume to get his attention, do it by clapping your hands, not by raising your voice. Go ahead then and get him to the prescribed toilet area and stand by quietly while he finishes the job he started inside. This should end up being a situation no different from any other call of nature for him.

Afterwards, clean the soiled area thoroughly with an odor neutralizer or some other odor-killing product. Make sure you clean it well, not only for your own olfactory satisfaction, but because your dog's sense of smell is many times greater than yours. If that spot remains smelling like a toilet area to him, he'll continue to use it as one. In addition, don't clean up the mess in front of your dog. He shouldn't get the idea that you're somehow his personal valet.

Finding an Unwanted Surprise

If you come in the room and find a mess on the floor, don't get mad. We know that's difficult. It's like someone telling you not to perspire when you're hot. Maybe you can't help mutter about the ill-starred ancestry of the little thug who left his calling card in the living room. One thing that may help you restrain yourself is to stop for a minute and realize why it happened: Somebody wasn't supervising him. Remember, your puppy or your new dog doesn't know what's going on yet. It's your job to assume the responsibility for teaching him if you want results.

Even with that in mind it can sometimes be maddening to find these little surprises in the least desirable places possible. "Why does he want to use the formal dining room of all places? It's the cleanest, most formal spot in the whole blasted house."

Again, pull back a bit and try to see things through your puppy's eyes, and you'll come to realize that he didn't choose that spot to relieve himself because he knew that it would get the biggest rise out of you. Think about it. It's the formal dining room. Nobody ever goes in there. It's quiet and undisturbed, and it's far away from any of the normal household activities.

In the wild, canines get as far away from the den as they reasonably can to relieve themselves. That's what your puppy was doing, too. In fact, given the circumstances, your puppy did the best he could. He went as far away from the den as he could so that he could avoid using his normal living area as a toilet. Almost makes you proud of him, doesn't it? Nevertheless, that sort of thing can't happen again. His good intentions don't make his behavior acceptable.

So, what do you do about it? This may sound a bit strange, but bear with me for a minute. Put your dog on a leash and calmly bring him to the scene of the crime. Remember, you're *not* mad at him. Keep your dog to your side, but not in front of you.

While he's watching what's going on, quickly and very firmly scold the mess on the floor. Yes, that's right: Scold the mess on the floor. Do not scold your dog. With a paper towel, blot up some of the mess and take both it and your dog out to the toilet area. Place the towel on the ground, and with your dog watching praise the messy towel for being in the proper place. Then just leave the towel where it is. What's going on here is that you are reinforcing the idea that the mess should be in the toilet area, not anywhere else. Words are being associated with both places and things.

For many of you, housetraining is an absolute must. It takes time and patience, but the rewards are well worth pursuing. What you're doing when you're housetraining is putting words to behavior, setting up schedules that will allow for success, being vigilant in supervising your dog so he won't make mistakes, and being consistent about all of the above. Throughout this process, it's important to your success that you train and monitor your dog in an understanding, empathetic and considerate manner. You'll get the best results that way, no matter what you're trying to teach.

Conclusion

As you've seen, creating and maintaining obedience in your dog, or your kids, can be rather involved. The alternatives to obedience aren't very appealing, so you've got work ahead of you. However, even though you've just been presented with a lot of information, if you can keep in mind the basic qualities of creating and maintaining obedience, you'll do just fine.

Above anything else, you must establish and then maintain your leadership role. If you don't do this, you can count on your attempts at training for obedience to fail. Your pack will not listen to you, so they will have no reason to do what you want them to do. You must insist on obedience because you are the leader. As the leader, you know what's right for everyone.

Create a structured life for your dog and your kids. Rules and routines lead to comfort and stability. Make sure that everyone knows what the rules are, and then abide by them always. You must be both consistent and constant in your insistence on obedience.

Finally, work toward generalizing obedience. Obedience on a here-and-there basis isn't going to work. If that's the way it goes, then when the chips are down and you most want obedience, you likely won't get it. Constancy in your insistence on obedience will work toward generalizing that obedience. Once commands are generalized, truly generalized, you can expect obedience in any setting and in any situation.

Part III
Behavior & Behaviorism

Introduction

If you see behavior in your dog you disapprove of, a natural inclination is to take your dog to a professional trainer and have that behavior trained away. The motivation behind seeking professional help is a good one: You're concerned about the dog's welfare or about your neighborhood or maybe your own sanity. There is nothing wrong with that.

The real problem is that many people who bring their dogs to our Academy don't understand what is actually involved in training. As a result, they don't fully understand the importance of their involvement with their dogs and how that involvement affects their dogs' behavior, either positively or negatively. This is why we train the owners of dogs and why we encourage them to interact with their dogs as they would in a parent-child relationship.

Many owners want a "microwave fix." They want to know, in as few words from us as possible: How can I fix my dog so that he never does this unwanted behavior again? Their desire for a quick fix is understandable. Most people bring their dogs in because a certain unwanted behavior has been going on for too long, and they're ready to start tearing their hair out if it doesn't stop—and stop fast. Unfortunately, the quick fix is rarely available, and even if they manage to control a negative behavior in their dogs relatively quickly, many clients still don't understand that the undesirable behavior could resurface if they don't maintain that control. There is the persistent belief among many dog owners that training is a form of surgery to remove an unwanted problem—they go in the one time, cut out that unwanted behavior, and that's that. Then they go home and live happily ever after. As we've seen along the way, that's simply not the case, for at least two important reasons.

For one, you can't simply cut out behavior like you would an appendix that's giving you trouble. You can't train away problem behavior, because more often than not, your dog's behavior is dependent on a number of things that lie beyond or outside training. To train a dog is to be a mechanic, or an instructor of mechanics. You can teach your dog the mechanics of sit, down, heel and hundreds of other command responses, but what happens if your dog eats the couch every time you leave the house? That is a problem with his behavior, and you need to go beyond mere training if you hope to correct it. You can't train away something like that because it's not a mechanical problem. Training is teaching your dog the mechanics for performing, but your dog's behavior is dependent on more than just his understanding of the mechanics of a command and the appropriate response to it.

The second reason why training can't produce a quick fix for negative behavior is that, even though training builds a foundation for obedience, it's an on-going process. You don't simply learn a particular training technique, apply it a few times, and then walk away from your dog expecting his undying obedience forever after.

We actually had a client ask: "Where do I hit my dog to get him to obey?" She must have thought there was some sort of off button somewhere on her dog that she needed to punch every so often to stop unwanted behavior. Apparently, she hadn't found it yet and was impatient to know where it was located.

Rather than give her a brief course on canine physiology, we tried to tell her that it doesn't work that way. Compare parenting your kids to parenting your dog and you'll know the reason in an instant. Very few people are silly enough to think they can take their kids through a month-long training session when they're two or three years old and then walk away from them because they're fixed forever. You can't expect to ship them off for a training session, no matter how long, and get your kids back, thinking: Oh, good. They'll mind me now and for the rest of their lives. No, they won't. Why should they? Amazingly, though, that's just what many people expect from having their dogs trained: Please fix my dog. I'll be back in a month. It doesn't work that way.

Training builds a foundation for obedience by helping your dog understand what it you want from him. However, whether or not he does what you want is another thing entirely. His behavior, not just his response to a given command, is dependent on a great many things in addition to his ability to recognize a command.

That's why you have to parent your dog. He wants to know who is at the helm. The teacher can teach some of the things they need to know, but it's your parenting and leadership skills that will guide them through their daily lives. A school teacher may convince your kids to obey in the classroom, and to exhibit behaviors consistent with classroom policy, but what happens when your kids come home? Do they just naturally think that the same rules and behaviors are in effect there, too? Your dog doesn't, and your kids may not either. The training the teacher gave them likely isn't going to be a quick fix for what's going on at home. Besides, everything's different at home: It's a different environment, the pack is made up of different members, and different things are occurring. If your dogs or your kids are going to obey you, and not just the school teacher, you're going to have to be a teacher, too. However, in your case, class doesn't get out at 2:30 in the afternoon. It's going on all the time, and parenting is the only way to meet the challenge. You may know how to parent your kids, but you're going to have to parent your dog, too. If you don't, no amount of training will allow you to alter many of his behaviors.

Me *ALPHA*...You *BETA*!

Chapter 6
Behaviors & Pack Dynamics

Being a good parent is dependent on a great many things. Some of these we've already talked about: assuming responsibility of leadership, creating a structured life for your dog and your kids, being consistent about following the rules, remaining constant in your responsibilities, and insisting on obedience at all times. But, being a good parent is also a matter of knowing what's going on with your family. Sometimes you'll see a change in a family member, maybe a change for the worse, but not know what caused it. It's at times like these that you want to determine the root of the problem so you can deal with it. Sometimes, though, you can't figure it out, especially if the family member in question isn't talking. Other times, the change in that family member is so alarming that you're afraid to deal with it on your own. In either case, your best bet is to seek out the advice of professionals.

If you're parenting your dog, the same things are likely going to happen with him. Sometime his behavior may change, seemingly all of a sudden, and you want to understand what caused that change so you can do something about it. This is a bit tricky since your dog isn't inclined to talk to you in ways you can always understand. Similarly, sometimes the changes in behavior that occur in your dog are so alarming that you figure you'd better get some professional help—like when your dog starts becoming aggressive. No sense in you or somebody else getting bit when you can get some help. Besides, why is he acting like that, anyway? He never used to.

Knowing what's behind unwanted or confusing behavior in your dog can help you correct it. But, it's a tricky matter determining the cause of a strange shift in your dog's behavior. Like the dog who lost his car, you can't always connect certain things with your dog's behavior because you're not trained to see and understand things the way your dog does. Even the "pros" aren't necessarily infallible at understanding behavioral shifts or problems in your dog.

This book can't tell you how to be a canine behaviorist. What it can do is provide some insight into things that may cause unwanted behavior in your dog. You may also understand the limitations involved with training your dog. Above all, we hope you come to see how your dog understands and reacts to the world around him. If you do, maybe you'll end up being a better parent for him.

Throughout this book, we've referred to your family as a pack. We've done so because that's how your dog sees you and your other family members. Because he sees your family like this, it's important that you realize that what goes on in your family affects him. All your interactions as a family—even ones that don't appear to involve your dog directly—are understood by him in terms of pack behavior. As a result, things going on in your family that seemingly don't concern your dog, really do concern him. After all, he is part of the pack.

When confronted with evidence of this for the first time, you may be amazed. You probably find it hard to believe that some new behavior that started showing up in your dog had something to do with what is going on in the pack as a unit.

When the dynamics of the pack are involved, so is your dog. At the Academy, one of the first things we do is an evaluation, in which parents and other family members discuss the problem they're having with their dog. In many instances, this is when we discover that the dog is fine, but pack dynamics are troubled.

As an example, consider the case of the client who came in with her eight-year-old daughter and her Boxer puppy. The puppy had recently bitten the girl, so the mother had wisely brought the dog in for professional help. As our conversation continued, it seemed as if we weren't getting enough information, and we could pry only so much before someone told us to mind our own business. They were talking, but not communicating. After awhile, the girl started misbehaving. She started sniping at her mother, and her mother sniped right back at her, and soon the girl and her mother really started going at one another. While this was embarrassing, it was also enlightening. The interaction between mother and daughter provided clues to what was going on with their dog, clues that we would never have been able to get just by asking. How do you ask someone: By the way, do you and your daughter fight a lot, and is your dog involved in those fights? We soon discovered, after their tantrums had died down, that the Boxer had an excellent temperament. We worked him, and he was a great little dog, stable and eager to please. However, the pack he lived with seemed to have major problems. When the mother and daughter argued, the girl would vent her frustrations on the only pack member smaller than herself— the puppy. For his part, the little Boxer could only take so much and then would defend himself. This problem dog had no problem at all, except for his pack.

Several important things can be learned from this particular case. First, here's a problem behavior in a dog that no amount of training could ever solve. Nothing anyone could do with that dog, short of breaking his spirit, would ever allow him to submit to that girl's abuse. Training should never attempt to solve such a situation, unless behavioral modification is directed at the relationship between the mother and daughter, and that option wasn't available to us.

Second, this is a good example of an emerging behavior in a dog caused, not by something within the dog, by what was going on in the larger pack. Mother and daughter couldn't get along. The dog was concerned about pack leadership because of the obvious challenges to that leadership exhibited by the daughter. The dog was uncomfortable about the pack's welfare. Another pack member was lashing out at him for no apparent reason.

He was confused and agitated, and the only thing he could do was defend himself until the pack leader re-established control and order. His behavior should have been expected, based on the sort of pack he had to try to fit into. There wasn't much hope of us helping mother and daughter get along, but we could help the dog. In this case, it worked out well for him. The parents decided that we were right, and he was placed with a more stable pack.

Whatever happens with you or other family members influences your dog's behavior, whether you realize it or not. He's a part of the family, too. Even if you feel you're not dealing directly with him in some matter, or that something shouldn't be a problem for him, he's likely going to sense that something is going on that should concern him.

As an example, a client with a parti-color Cocker Spaniel sought help because the dog was acting strange whenever she left the house. We mention the color of the dog because we have observed over the years that certain behaviors can be fairly accurately assigned to color variations in certain breeds. For example, if someone told us that a certain Cocker was biting people, our first thought would be that it was buff-colored. Even though the parti-color Cocker seems to exhibit the least problematic temperament of the color types for this breed, we had seen nervous behavior in other parti-color Cockers before. As a result, we were mentally prepared to find a problem dog.

The client was worried about her dog. She had selected the dog because she lived in a condo and the board of directors had told her that a Cocker Spaniel was one of the acceptable breeds because of its size. Although a Cocker wasn't this woman's first choice in a dog, she wanted a dog and this was her first choice among those permitted. This was a sweet, little dog, and he had the sort of face that would melt your heart. But, things weren't working out. The dog went crazy whenever she left him on his own in the condo. He would whine and yap all day, and she was getting complaints. She loved this little dog, and she wanted to overcome the dog's fears of being left alone.

This seemed like an odd situation. The woman had owned her Cocker for quite some time, but she said that she was only now getting complaints about his behavior. Asked if his whining and fear of being on his own was a very recent development, she said that, yes, it was. Very recent. That was odd. We asked her questions about her dog's environment at the condo: Had things changed there recently. We kept asking and asking but couldn't come up with anything that looked like it could have sparked this new behavior in her dog. Above all, it seemed odd to us that she had owned the dog for so long but hadn't experienced this sort of behavior in him until just recently.

Finally, we went back to square one: "Tell us about how your dog acted in the past when you'd leave him on his own."

"Well, my parents said that he was always just fine with them."

"Your parents? What do you mean?"

"Well, whenever I had to go out I always dropped him off at my parents house until I could get back. I didn't want him to be on his own, you see. But, they said he was always just fine with them. Now my parents have moved and I can't do that anymore."

Ah ha! So that's what's going on here. The woman had decided that her Cocker didn't like to be left alone, and so whenever she left the house she dropped him off at her parents' place and then picked him up on the way back. That way he was never alone which caused serious separation issues between her and her dog. She had inadvertently created a little monster who absolutely refused to be left alone.

But, there was more going on. She started to tell me about certain cruel veterinarians she had taken her dog to see. Whenever the vet began to perform some examination procedure, the little Cocker squealed a bit—Cockers do that sort of thing—the woman would fall apart. Based on her own descriptions, she simply came unglued when she thought the vet was roughing up her little puppy. She immediately switched vets because she didn't want her puppy to have negative associations with going to see the vet. That told us more, but there were still some missing pieces to the puzzle.

As we sat discussing her dog, we noticed that the Cocker had never once left her lap during our entire conversation. Nor did she seem willing to let him leave even if the dog had been so inclined. We had seen negative behaviors in dogs generated by that sort of relationship before, so we knew it was time for some serious talking.

"Just for a minute, let's talk about how you might want to raise a child someday. Wouldn't you want to help your child feel confident and competent?"

"Naturally. Of course."

"Similarly, you wouldn't want your child to be afraid of everything, would you?"

She understood what we were driving at, but she had to answer that, no, she wouldn't want her child to be fearful of everything.

"Think about it," we said. "And, think about how that relates to your dog. With your child, you have to start working toward building a personality into something that would allow happiness, not paranoia. Even though you did what you thought was best for protecting your puppy, what you really did was build paranoia and fear. You're doing it right now. You're in a new place with new people and you're afraid of something happening to your dog. And when you're afraid, you're teaching him to be afraid. Paranoia is not fun to live with, whether you're a child or a puppy."

By the look on her face, she was even afraid of what we'd just told her. We removed her dog and started to work with him. The woman was impressed with the way we handled him, but all we were doing was giving the dog the chance to stand on his own, away from his pack leader. He did well. Finally, we took his leash and looped it around a doorknob so we could sit and talk without distraction.

The Cocker was only three feet away from her and was handling things just fine, but as we talked the woman kept glancing back repeatedly at her dog. She grew progressively more anxious and agitated. Finally, she came out with it all. She described how she had come from a dysfunctional family and that now that she's on her own she's having a hard time coping. She didn't want to be alone, but she was afraid of anything that might upset her chances of making it on her own. The last piece of the puzzle slid into place: she was communicating her own separation and abandonment fears to her dog.

We never intended that session to be therapy for her, but as it turned out, that's what it was, and that's how we figured out how she could help her dog—by helping herself. She had an opportunity to help her dog by examining the things she didn't like in herself. On the other hand, she had the opportunity to create a mirror image of herself in her dog. We don't know which option she took. But, when she left, she seemed to have more confidence in herself than when she first walked through the door.

Pack dynamics, particularly those that involve the leadership of the pack or the way the pack is structured, are going to influence your dog's behavior. In packs with strong leadership and with stable structures, this influence is going to be positive. However, if leadership waivers or changes occur in the pack, this influence can negatively affect your dog's behavior.

A man who was a professional bodyguard called us for help. He had provided personal protection for celebrities all over the world for much of his adult life. He was big, strong and intelligent. Nobody pushed this guy around. The only information he relayed over the phone was that he and his wife were having problems with their dog. When they showed up with their five-year-old Boxer, she refused to get out of the car. Apparently, she had decided she was staying in the car and that was final. The couple tried coaxing her out, but the Boxer just snorted and refused to budge. They were embarrassed by this, and they told us that maybe they should try to come another time.

We told them they shouldn't do that, and that we'd get her out of the car one way or another and finally managed to coax her out. Then we started fact finding.

For the past three years, each evening as the man sat in his chair, the Boxer would growl at him if he decided to move. She would give a threatening growl if he moved at all. But, if he actually tried to get out of the chair, she'd attack him.

Every night this burly bodyguard was literally trapped in his chair. Once, he tried to make a dash for the television remote control and then jump back in his chair, but he couldn't move fast enough. The Boxer came flying across the room and laid into him. Not only was this a dangerous situation, it was also hard on this fellow's ego. He had always thought of himself as a fairly tough guy who never let others push him around, and now his own dog was making him a prisoner in his own chair.

They also had problems with visitors coming to the house. As soon as guests arrived, and everybody was settled, they were all trapped in their chairs. This behavior couldn't be tolerated any longer.

The situation reminded us of Attila and his first owner. Perhaps this was a leadership issue as it was in Attila's case, or maybe something else was going on that was causing the dog to assume control of the rest of the pack. We never found out for certain what was causing this behavior, but we were able to do something about it.

Don't anyone move!

The solution was rather simple. The Boxer never exhibited aggressive behavior until after people were seated, so as a first step we put a leash on her and tied her to a doorknob before we all sat down. That way she couldn't attack us. Then, we got up, moved around, sat back down and got up again. As you can probably guess, the dog was frustrated about the whole thing. She obviously wanted to come over and get us back in our chairs and have us stay put, but she couldn't. We then praised her for this new—albeit involuntary—restrained behavior. This routine was repeated over and over. In time, the dog came to understand that restraint was going to be insisted on, no matter what. She was eventually allowed to try restraining herself off-leash, and she was fine.

Whenever changes occur in the pack, your dog is going to become concerned. To you, those changes may or may not seem important, but whatever they are, they're going to influence how your dog behaves. At the Academy we've had clients with mopey dogs, agitated dogs, nervous dogs, aggressive dogs and dogs that have suddenly taken up urinating in the house.

Many of those dogs came had one thing in common: A member of the pack had left. Bobby or Suzy had gone off to college, or there'd been a death in the family or the parents had separated or divorced. Change in the pack is not a good thing for your dog. The entire pack mechanism is designed to create stability and the comfort that comes from it. Once that stability is threatened, your dog becomes uncomfortable.

Other things are at work when a pack member leaves your pack: People are sad, angry, confused, etc. Your dog is attuned to those things, and they influence him. When tragedy strikes the pack, such as divorce, separation, or death, emotions are heightened. Your dog senses that. He may become confused or agitated, and the loss of comfort from the loss of stability may bring out undesirable behavioral changes in him.

If it is the pack leader who's left, your dog is going to feel either hopelessly confused about what he's supposed to do or he may try to take over the pack leadership position.

Many people have more than one dog, but many of these people don't come by all their dogs at the same time. They have one and then they get another; then maybe another. Just like subtractions to the pack, additions to it change the overall dynamics of the pack. Dogs need to test each other to see where they stand in the pack now that the pack has changed. One dog may suddenly begin to show greater aggressiveness than he had in the past, because then he didn't feel a challenge to his position, and now he does.

Or, if that new pack member, perhaps a cute little puppy, suddenly becomes the center of the pack's attention and affection, you may find your other dog moping around or off his feed. His place in the pack has been usurped by this little upstart, even if you didn't mean for that to happen. If the new addition is a child, you may see your dog acting pushy towards him. The dog is trying to establish or maintain his position in the pack with this newcomer, just as he would with the addition of another dog.

Other changes in pack dynamics or its members may affect your dog's behavior. Boys entering puberty may find themselves at odds with an adult male dog, because he senses a possible challenge to his male role in the pack. We've seen behavioral changes in a family's dog resulting from a family member involved with drug use. To the dog, the person was suddenly acting strange, and that made the dog uncomfortable. The parents were concerned about their dog's sudden display of discomfort whenever their child came in the room, and while they suspected that he was involved with drugs, they made no connection between that and their dog's behavior.

When a client returned after a month to get his male Rottweiler, Baron, the dog sniffed him and growled and didn't seem to recognize him at all. However, everyone at the Academy anticipated this reaction, or lack of it. Baron's owner had been ill, in the hospital, and still taking antibiotics. Antibiotics alter body chemistry, and as a result, alter your base smell. Baron's owner didn't smell right to him. He had changed somehow.

Dogs do not like change, either in the way the pack is set up, or in its members. Anything that can influence the pack can potentially influence your dog's behavior. When troubles afflict the pack your dog's behavior can be affected. He's a member of your pack, and it's in his own best interests when the pack is running smoothly.

Chapter 7
Unconscious Reinforcement
of Negative Behavior

Changes in the pack structure or its members aren't the only things that influence your dog's behavior. Your own actions and decisions—even unconscious ones—can create negative behavior or create an environment in which negative behavior may grow and flourish.

Many times, this is the result of your misunderstanding of what you really want from your dog, or what you want out of a dog in general. For some people, a dog is intended to be a part of their image. It's like the person who buys a flashy sports car to project a particular image. Some of those people just aren't sports car types. They discover that their choice in vehicles isn't working out: "How the heck am I going to haul firewood in my Ferrari?" The same thing can happen when people choose a certain breed of dog. They may find out that their own personalities or habits don't match the dogs they get.

If possible, you should view a litter of puppies before selecting the particular one you want. This is always a good idea, because certain traits you see in a puppy are likely going to be ones that will remain with him for the rest of his life. Unfortunately, you sometimes become attracted to a particular dog for all the wrong reasons.

We ask people why they picked a particular dog or a particular breed of dog to understand their intentions for owning a dog at all, and also to see what sort of expectations they have for living with their dogs. The responses we get often reveal why an owner is experiencing problems with his dog. Assertiveness seems to attract many people to a particular puppy in a litter.

"Why did you pick this particular puppy?" we'll ask. "Well, this was the one that really stood out from the rest. He was racing around. When they opened the gate he took off at a dead run after the birds, so I thought 'Wow, that's one spunky little dog!'" That's fine if you intend to share a spunky life with your dog, but if you're a dedicated couch potato, you'd better expect either a maddening relationship with your dog, or a dog that is very unhappy about his life with you. If he's unhappy, expect problem behaviors from him.

We often run into spunky-and-the-spud relationships. Sometimes the spud will get a spunky dog because he thinks that will encourage him to change his habits: "Boy, with a dog like that I'd be getting out every day for a lot of good exercise!" Be realistic. Have you ever bought exercise equipment thinking that doing so will help motivate changes in your habits or lifestyle? A dog can't simply be stored away someplace like a treadmill once you discover you're really not as motivated for exercise as you hoped you'd be.

If you're thinking about getting a high-energy dog, think about what you're getting into. If you can't accommodate his need to burn off that energy, you're creating a situation in which the potential for problem behavior will escalate. Why is he digging up the back yard or tearing after the neighbor's kids? It could be that he's just plain bored and needs to burn off exess energy somehow.

People often have unrealistic expectations of their future relationship with their dogs, and as a result create a mismatch of personalities. Sometimes people get dogs with specific goals in mind, but don't have a sense of what their dogs are supposed to do when not engaged in the tasks they were bred to perform.

We often see this, and the problems it can create, in people who select hunting breeds. The person who gets a dog to use his hunting skills may have unrealistic expectations. The person who only hunts two or three times a year finds that he's got a dog that is useless, as far as he's concerned, the rest of the time. Instead of an exciting, satisfied life filled with doing things hundreds of years of breeding have trained him to do, the dog finds himself living outside, chained, waiting for those few special moments when he can truly live. He's dirty, so he doesn't get to come inside much. He's bored, so he's excavating pit-mines in the back yard. He becomes ill-mannered and barks at nothing in particular. Somehow, he doesn't seem like much fun. In fact, he seems like a real pest most of the time, and he only earns his keep a few times a year. Even then, when he's finally out in the field, he's out of control with excitement. This problem dog doesn't have a problem. His problem is that he got stuck with someone who couldn't or wouldn't do with him what he was bred to do.

There's no reason why you can't have a hunting dog as a member of your family—truly a member. If you're involved with competition and you're hunting your dog hard, many times a week, you might get away with leaving him outside for those short periods when he wasn't actively working with you. But, many of you are seasonal hunters at best, active during fall and early winter, and then hanging up your boots for nine months of the year. Some seasons it seems like too many things come along and you end up saying: "Well, I didn't get out as much this year as I would have liked to."

If you select a working dog, you should make that dog a member of your family. Have him inside with you, with the person who most often works him being the primary caregiver. Your dog will not understand why he is an outcast from the pack if you constantly leave him outside away from you. He wants to be with you, the pack, and having him with you is the best way to train him and maintain that training.

Teaching him house manners—things that you teach him apart from his specialized, work-oriented training—will help him become more integrated with the larger pack. It will also help him be a more effective worker for you. He'll be happier, more comfortable with his role in the pack, and will be able to see you as the real pack leader—not just someone who comes around every so often and tries to get him to do something. His role as a true pack member will allow him to be calmer and more respectful of you as pack leader, and as a result he will be a better-mannered, more respectful and effective working dog.

You can't expect obedience or respect from an outcast family member. Parents who find themselves too much away from home, always on business trips or too involved with getting things done, likely also find interacting with their children difficult. It's an intermittent relationship at best.

Although it was unintentional, children may feel that dad (or mom) doesn't really want them around. They don't feel like true members of the family, because the family is never really there. When that happens, those family members may not be as receptive to things as you'd like them to be. They might begin to think: Who is this guy, anyway? That's going to happen with your hunting dog, too. Even if you've worked hard on his field training, if he doesn't feel like he's part of your pack, he's going to have a hard time seeing you as his leader. He's going to develop unwanted behavior in your absence, because you weren't around to do anything about it.

You may misunderstand your dog's temperament, and your

interactions with him may cause, usually unintentionally, unwanted behaviors. You create a mismatch of temperaments between you and your dog.

Observing a puppy's behavior during a temperament test can be a valuable tool for evaluating what sort of dog you're going to have when the puppy grows up. While the information that comes from such a test isn't infallible, you can still learn a lot about your puppy's behavior from a professional analysis. Temperament tests focus on a puppy's attitude toward people, noise sensitivity, reaction to changes, pain threshold, retrieving ability, dominance, confidence, independence and/or shyness. These traits are clear indications of what the puppy's personality will probably be like as he grows older. Because of this, a professional can help match you with the appropriate dog for your personality and lifestyle.

Without professional insight, people often see a particular behavior in a puppy, draw the wrong conclusions about what that behavior means for the future, and end up bringing home the wrong dog. For example, adoption of a very sensitive dog by some big, gruff guy whose method of greeting both man and beast includes a hearty whack along with a blustery, "Hi! How are ya," is a disaster waiting to happen. The poor dog will always feel threatened and the owner will be disappointed by his very timid dog. On the other hand, a puppy who is impervious to pain is going to run roughshod over the owner who thinks putting a leash on a dog is unnecessarily cruel.

Having some sense of what a certain breed of dog was bred for, as well as what an individual dog's personality is going to be like, will help you make good decisions when trying to find the dog that's right for you. If getting a dog is an impulsive move on your part, or you don't take the time to educate yourself about the type of dog you are getting, you are setting yourself up for the possibility of having to parent a problem child.

Consider the case of Sydney. Sydney was an Australian Cattle Dog, a cute, little, reddish puppy. We first saw him when he was about eight or nine weeks old and just an adorable little dog. This was a case in which the whole family came in for his evaluation, so I knew he was a family dog. The first thing we asked them was where they had gotten him. They replied they had purchased him from a breeder.

"Why did you pick an Australian Cattle Dog?" we asked. They had been on summer vacation in Montana and had seen two Cattle Dogs at the ranch where they had stayed. These were working dogs on the ranch, and it was easy for the family to see how phenomenal these dogs were while on the job. They're smart, medium-sized, strong, low-maintenance dogs who handle a tough environment with little concern. If you ever have a chance to see this breed at work, you will walk away with admiration for them. Besides, they're very adaptable, even to city life, and as far as this family was concerned, they were just the right size for their own home and yard environment. But then, these folks had only seen these dogs in their working environment.

This was a predicament. We didn't want to tell them what kinds of problems they were likely to have from a working breed like this who wasn't working all the time; we didn't want them to start seeing ghosts in their dog's behavior, or they might create unwanted behavior by trying to avoid doing certain things with him. On the other hand, we knew they needed to be cautioned about the potential for certain problems so they wouldn't blunder into them because they didn't understand what this particular breed is like.

If you travel in Eastern Washington, you'll find that quite a few farmers and ranchers have Australian Cattle Dogs because this is a dog who can handle a tough working load. At public gatherings, you often see row after row of pickup trucks, and nearly every one will have a dog in the back. Most of those dogs will be a working cattle dog—Border Collies, Australian Shepherds, and so on. But, one thing is for sure, if there's an Australian Cattle Dog in the pickup, you should keep your distance. Everyone in Eastern Washington knows this.

You don't mess with these dogs when they're looking out for their owners' turf. If you get bitten by one, you were someplace you shouldn't have been—it's that simple. If an owner of an Australian Cattle Dog needs something out of his truck, he has to get it himself because nobody else will be allowed to get near the truck. With anyone else's dog you'd just go over, ask him to move aside, take what you need and get on with your business. Not with these guys, though.

So, here's this family, mom and dad and four little kids, sitting in front of us and alarms were going off. We explained that when Australian Cattle Dogs bite, they don't just nip at you to say, "Get out of my face." They *bite*. We tried to tell them what sort of life these dogs were bred for to make them understand what they were in for. These dogs are one of the better "chute dogs" among cattle dogs around the world. These are dogs that can go into a cattle chute where things are tight and dangerous and hold their own with angry, unpredictable animals that outweigh them by 1,500 pounds. These are amazingly tough dogs. There are plenty of good herding breeds around, but most of them don't make good chute dogs. Australian Cattle Dogs can get in there and mix it up with those big brutes, and they don't earn respect by merely nipping at a steer's heels.

Our next question was: "Would you tell us about your neighborhood?" We were hoping they live out in the boondocks that's only reachable by snowmobile and climbing gear. Not a chance. Their neighborhood was full of families and little kids.

The best we could do right then was warn them. We told them the choice they'd made for a dog was about as bad as it could get. They had invited a tough, little, high-energy dog into their home, and it was good money that when something upset him for any reason, somebody was going to get bitten.

However, now that they had made their choice, they were determined to stick with it. They were convinced they could handle this sweet, little puppy as he grew older. While we had to admire their determination, we also had much to be concerned about. They attended our training classes and worked at doing all they could to make life with Sydney a good one.

By the time Sydney was eight months old, the family had reached the point where, if their kids had any friends over, which was frequently, they'd tie Sydney to the bedpost. That was a bad thing to do. If you isolate your dog when company comes over, he soon becomes very resentful of newcomers. To his way of thinking, it's *their* fault that he gets tied up whenever they come around. He's not going to be happy with company as a result.

Well, there's poor Sydney tied to the bedpost just about every day, and he's positively brimming with resentment. One day, he broke his lead and immediately attacked a neighbor boy. The family called us, very concerned about what they could do to make the situation better. Unfortunately, there really wasn't much they could do, not in their current situation, and we told them so.

As a rule, we don't take in many dogs when they don't work out with clients. But, with Sydney we felt a particular obligation because we'd watched him grow up. His family had made a determined effort to train him properly, and none of what was going on with him was really his fault. His family had chosen the wrong breed of dog. We had Sydney for a short while, but our own situation with an Australian Cattle Dog wasn't much better. We were going to be forced to put him down because of our dangerous situation with clients coming and going all the time, and there's a lot of insurance liability that goes with a dog like that.

As it turned out, a friend of ours from Eastern Washington came to visit. When our friend arrived he saw Sydney. He lived out on a farm and had older kids and lots of room. We realized that this was a totally different situation from the one Sydney had been in before—

G'day, mate!..*Don't even think of touching this truck!*

perfect for an Australian Cattle Dog. He took Sydney back home and things worked out great. This is one of those times when the story has a happy ending. Our friend calls us with new stories about Sydney and his life on the farm—he just adores that dog. But, you know what? Nobody can get in his pickup truck!

Misunderstanding a dog's temperament can lead to big problems. This is often the case with people who get so-called personal protection dogs. You wouldn't believe the number of people at the Academy with dogs purchased with personal protection in mind, and whose relationship with their dogs have turned sour.

These are usually dogs that act tough, snapping, barking and growling at everybody that passes by. These dogs aren't safe to be around because they are out of control. What appears to be toughness in their behavior is more often the result of fear and confusion. These dogs are called fear-biters; that is, they lash out at others because of their lack of confidence and their fears. When a dog is afraid, he's not thinking. As a result, they are out of control, and can't effectively protect themselves, let alone have the presence of mind to protect someone else effectively and responsibly.

The most important characteristic of a personal protection dog is absolute obedience, along with evidence that the dog is able to exercise judgment when his owner is either threatened or incapacitated. Try this little test to see if your dog is ready to start personal protection training. Put your dog in a down stay. If anyone can get him up off this command without your personal release, the dog isn't ready to begin protection training. Your dog must be obedient to the point where, if he is airborne attacking an intruder and you say, "Stop!" the dog immediately and without hesitation drops to the ground, never touching his intended target.

People who want a dog to watch their cars or houses and trust to keep an eye on things while they're away is an acceptable and proper use of these specialty dogs. But, even in these situations, obedience and absolute control through extensive training is a must. With some of the better protection dogs, it's difficult to get them to bite at all. Their intent is not to hurt people, but rather to control their actions.

A fellow who worked for a prominent Northwest newspaper owned a highly trained protection dog that had been taught by an authority on the subject. One evening, when he came home from work, he found his front door standing wide open. His first thought was: "Oh, brother! Here I spent all this money, worked with my dog all the time, and now I come home and..." His house was a shambles. Then he heard a voice in the kitchen calling out to him. He went to the kitchen and found a man crouched on top of the refrigerator and his guard dog sitting on the floor below intently watching him. The burglar pleaded with the man to call the police or anything, but please get that dog away from him! The dog had the man trapped, and he wasn't going anywhere. He hadn't hurt the burglar, but by the same token, the burglar knew he wasn't getting down off that refrigerator.

Behavioral problems in your dog can be the result of many different things. Sometimes, it's a problem in the pack, and other times it's a problem with the choice you make getting a dog. But, other things that you do with your dog, or don't do, can spark unwanted behavior.

Even nurturing your dog can bring on negative behavior, if it's done at the wrong times or to an excessive degree. Dogs are tough. If you spay a female dog, something that constitutes major surgery, the next day she'll be up and running around.

Dogs can handle things a lot better than people can, not because their pain tolerance is any greater, but because they're naturally inclined to be active and they force themselves to work through it.

Among people, you can watch a parent inadvertently encourage hypochondria in a child by rewarding illness. This isn't an exact parallel with dogs, since hypochondria requires abstract thought, but there are some similarities. During an illness, parents may inadvertently teach a child to be very good at bossing them around.

The child learns that he can demand almost anything and be waited on hand and foot because he's not feeling well. Then, when he's feeling better, it's still, "Bring me this!" The parents have taken themselves out of their leadership roles and put themselves in subservient ones. That's not what the patient needs. The patient needs to be cared for, but cared for by a leader who lovingly, but firmly, maintains his position of authority.

We've seen true problem dogs grow out of situations in which the dog was ill or injured for a time and was not merely cared for, but absolutely babied. The parents unconsciously created a monster who grew to learn from them that he could have anything he wanted, or be excused for any indiscretion. It was difficult for the dog's owners to understand that they were killing him with kindness. The world isn't a place in which you can get away with a bring-me-this attitude for very long. The dog learns that the pack leadership is weak and can be ignored.

Some people, though not nearly enough, rescue their dogs from a shelter. There's the tendency among people who do so to feel sorry for their new dogs and to overdo it with the nurturing. Before they know it, they have serious problems with their dog's lack of obedience. It's relatively rare to see dogs brought in by owners who obtained their dog through shelters that have also suffered abuse.

However, if you ask these people if they think their dogs had been abused, they often reply: "Yes, because he shrinks from my touch when I try to pet him." While that might be a sign of prior abuse, more often it's simply indicative of a dog with a submissive nature. However, the owners of these same dogs tend to baby their dogs as a way of making it up to them for having lived through hard times. When that happens, their leadership roles become compromised and behavioral problems emerge.

Along the same lines as over nurturing is the tendency to be over-protective of your kids, both the two- and four-legged kind. Sometimes you end up rewarding negative behavior by fighting your children's battles for them. If you have a child who comes to you for comfort or rescue every time something goes wrong and is never given the opportunity to stand on his own, you're actually rewarding him for avoiding using his own initiative and resources to solve problems, and you're crippling his ability to cope with future adversity.

That's not your intention. Your intention is to make life easier and remove needless obstacles. However, the long-term message is more subtle than, "I'm trying to help you." It's really, "Oh, you poor thing. You'll never be capable of standing on your own; but, don't worry, I'll always be here to protect you." Do you want to see that kind of dependency in your child's future?

Now, let's look at it a different way. If you're sitting at home and somebody new walks in the door and your dog begins to shake and act nervous, he's probably scared. When this or something obviously frightening upsets your dog, your reaction might be to console him by petting him and saying, "It's okay; it's all right. There, you're good now."

What your dog is getting from this so-called consolation is actually praise. That's how you talk to him and treat him when he does something you like. He must be doing the right thing by being scared of these people coming into the room, because you're praising him. This must be exactly what you expect of him: Cringe when something new shows up and never work through the fear, because apparently fear is good. At least, that's what you're telling him.

Compare the same situation to the shy child who hides behind mom or dad. He's getting positive reinforcement for his lack of confidence; he's getting positive reinforcement to a negative behavior even though that is not what mom or dad would want for their child's long-term future. They're doing it unknowingly. They're teaching him that this behavior is perfectly acceptable because they allow it to continue. They're saying: "It's fine for you to hide, because I'm here to protect you. You don't have to try to protect yourself, ever; I know you can't."

Naturally, if a child is afraid of the dark, you don't lock him in a dark room so he can experience true terror as a way of breaking through his fears, but neither do you baby him so that he learns that it's okay to be afraid of the dark. Instead, you work with the child, perhaps playing some games in low lighting and then progressing on to do the same in darkness as a means of working through his fears. If his behavior improves, you praise it; if it doesn't, you work to negate it, not allow it to continue.

Lots of people with dogs that exhibit fears of something—and no doubt lots of people with children in the same situation—simply try to avoid the things that triggers this fear rather than attempt to work through it. "Oh, we try to avoid getting too close to the lake. Our dog's scared to death of it." That's just great. Better lock Bozo in the car or leave him at home if you want to go fishing or take a walk along any body of water. "We can't leave Suzy by herself; she's afraid of being alone for even an instant!" Might as well get some handcuffs and link up for life, if you don't plan on working through such fears.

It can be difficult watching your youngster trying to cope with certain aspects of life. After all, your natural instinct is to nurture and protect, not disengage. But, if they're going to learn how to cope with those things, you've got to engage your kids in the right ways. Learning to work through these fears will eventually allow your dog or child to become an emotionally confident adult, able to handle the natural stresses that come with living.

They have to learn how to deal with life eventually. The longer they delay in doing so, the tougher it's going to be. If you bring us a dog who's scared of vacuum cleaners, you can bet he's going to see a lot of them during his stay with us, once you've established both control and trust with him. If you're a good pack leader at home for all your kids, one who does have control and trust, then you can work through fears in them, too, and avoid needlessly reinforcing those fears.

Dogs are both exceptionally tough and resilient and extremely sensitive. It's truly amazing what kinds of things your dog picks up on, and the kinds of things that affect him. Our dogs are extremely conscious of pain, not their own but ours. Whenever we hurt ourselves or are sick, at least one dog will rush over and lick us, trying to soothe our pain. They're not stupid. They know we hurt. They pick up on *everything*: your body language, your tone of voice, and your moods.

It may be difficult for you to understand sometimes just how sensitive your dog can be, particularly when something's going on that you just naturally assume doesn't involve him. Many times, what you're doing with your dog or, again, not doing with him, is a real influence on hisbehavior. This is clearly seen in the *Lady and the Tramp* Syndrome.

If for some reason your life has some serious pieces missing from it—like seeing Walt Disney films—we'll describe briefly the film from which this syndrome takes its name. Lady, a Cocker Spaniel, lives with a wonderful pair of human pack leaders. They love her and would do just about anything for her, and in return she loves them with undying devotion. Then, mom and dad have a baby. Lady thinks the baby is terribly nice, too, but she quickly finds that mom and dad don't have as much time for her as they did, because of the new arrival, and also that they're concerned about Lady being in the same room as the baby. Naturally, since they spend so much time with their baby, mom and dad keep Lady away from them much of the time now. If you have a dog, and have recently had a baby, does this description ring a bell?

New parents come to the Academy with dogs who have gotten caught in the Lady and the Tramp Syndrome. Many of them even understand what's going on with their dog. You wouldn't believe how many times we've heard the parental lament: "We've worked very hard to keep our dog as part of the family because we didn't want him to feel left out, but..." In the movie, and it's likely a similar situation for many in real life, Lady discovers that any time the baby is awake, she's sent away, but as soon as the baby falls asleep again, she receives love and praise. The movie dog isn't stupid, and neither is your dog. Pretty soon, she starts to make the connection: "Whenever the kid's around, I'm banished, but as soon as the kid's out of the picture, things are running smoothly for me again. Hmmmm."

Your dog makes the connection, too. His position in the pack, and all the attention and privileges that come with it, is being usurped through no fault of his own: "Hey! What about me? I've been good, right? I'm still doing all the things I'm supposed to, right? What's the deal here? Oh, it's the kid again, is it? Well, if I can't get your attention by doing the old things, I'll try something new. Let's start with the curtains."

For the most part, the parents are not intending to neglect their dog, it's just that their timing is all wrong. When the baby comes, WHAM, the dog's out of the picture, and this is a real shock. One good thing about the arrival of a baby in the house is that you've got plenty of forewarning.

When you know a baby is coming, start to cut back slowly on the amount of attention your dog is getting. About six weeks prior to the baby's arrival, try your best to ignore your dog. This is harder than it might seem, since during that period your instinct to nurture is going to be very strong. Hormones and feelings are running high at this time, and your dog very likely has always been the major object of these feelings.

When your baby does arrive, then shower him with attention whenever the baby is present. Pretty soon your dog is thinking: "I don't know what you did, kid, but you sure got things back to normal around here. I really gotta hand it to you." You may find that when that happens, a very strong show of affection from your dog is extended toward the child. And, if you've seen Disney films before, you know quite well that they all lived happily ever after.

One thing that you may fail to do that can create negative behavior is failing to spay or neuter your dog. Many people don't want to spay or neuter their dogs because they harbor the mistaken belief that it will somehow negatively alter personality or physical development. Nothing is further from the truth. Your dog will continue to develop normally and naturally.

We had someone tell us that when they had their dog neutered, he became depressed. They had owned their dog, a huge Newfoundland, for six years, but had him neutered at last because he roamed the neighborhood getting into fights with other dogs, raccoons, and anything else he bumped into. As a result, their vet bills were becoming a real burden. When we arrived, they called their dog and he came running up. They started to pet him and say, "Poor old, Chuckie. You lost your manhood, didn't you? Poor old guy..." and so on. Naturally, the dog lowered his ears and head and morosely slumped away. Later, we played with him and he was happy and lively and chased madly after every ball we threw for him. Chuckie himself had no problem with his neutering, but his owners did. They continually communicated their sadness to him—the way *they* would feel if *they* had been altered.

So, aside from avoiding adding to the members of death row at your local shelter, why *should* you spay or neuter your dog? What's that got to do with his behavior? When your dog comes into adolescence, it's not a slow, gradual process. Instead, it's WHAM! Here's your testosterone! Good luck! It is quite literally a flood of hormones in his system that completely throws his whole life out of kilter.

After this hefty dose of testosterone poisoning, his behavior is likely going to be manic at times; he's going to be marking everywhere, aggressively defending his territory, chasing off possible competition, and trying to breed with anything that moves.

If you neuter him, he'll still be a teenager, but you'll have a much better handle on his hormonally influenced behaviors. These behaviors won't be totally eliminated, mind you, but you'll be much more able to control them. When your dog becomes a victim of his own hormones and you've failed to establish effective controls, you may be in for some unpleasant surprises, particularly if you have one of the more powerful breeds, like a Rottweiler.

But, even if you have a less powerful or more passive breed, you may be still headed for trouble if you fail to neuter him. We had a client with a five-year-old male Yellow Labrador. The man said he was having all sorts of problems with him urinating in the house and being generally destructive. As a result, the Lab had been confined to the back yard. We said, "It sounds like he was originally a house dog. What changed?"

"Well, he's just urinating everywhere now. He's marked everything in the house and he just keeps right on doing it."

"That sounds like hormonal-based behavior," Why don't you have him neutered? That will help out a lot."

"I can't do that," he said.

"Why not?"

"Because his mother was a National Specialty Winner, so he's a really well-bred dog and I paid a lot of money for him."

We thought about that for a minute and then asked: "What has this particular dog done as far as competition is concerned?"

"Well, actually, nothing."

"How many people have come to you asking to use him as a stud dog?"

"None at all."

"Then why is he unneutered? Because his mother won the National Specialty? What has he, as an individual done? What are you doing to promote him if he's such a well-bred dog?"

While he was mulling that over, we said: "You need to be realistic about this. Your dog is now isolated in the back yard because of behavior which is the direct result of his being an unneutered male dog.

His life is miserable. He's showing you that it's miserable through the destructive behavior that's going on. All this because his mother won a dog show? Does that really make sense?"

Here was a dog that was being punished simply because his mother had won a ribbon. The owner had neither the time nor the skill to train his dog for the show ring; he would never win a scrap of paper, let alone a ribbon, and he was sentenced to a life of frustration and isolation.

If you know some dog breeders, do you see them keeping many

males intact? Not a chance. They want the female dogs that can be bred to make money, but they let somebody else cope with all the aggravation of the male marking everywhere and being aggressive.

In addition, your dog can't unlearn some of the things that his unneutered sex-drive indirectly teaches him. Say you've got an six-month-old puppy who hasn't yet been flooded with testosterone. He's willing to sit contentedly in the back yard, playing with toys, happy to be alive. Then, WHAM, he receives the hormonal surge. Suddenly, he notices an appealing female dog just down the street. Now, the dog that was once content to play in the back yard behind the fence, is going to break his neck to find a way out!

When he does get out, and he will because his drive is very strong to do so, not only does he find the agreeable female down the street, he also finds that the neighbors leave delicious bowls of cat food on their porch, plus, the kids down the street play ball every day at four o'clock, and it's really fun to play ball.

Well, you haul your dog back home, fix the fence, get him neutered, and you figure that's that. Well, your dog is no longer as interested in the little female dog that lives down the street, but there's still cat food on the porch next door, and the kids down the block are still playing ball. Your dog's horizons have been expanded, and they won't shrink back. He'll still be highly motivated to get beyond that fence.

We often have people question the idea of spaying a female dog, too. They understand all about the problems with an unneutered male, but why should they get their female spayed? After all, she only comes in season once or twice a year. True enough, but the hormonal influence on female dogs can create serious aggression problems. Many females tend to become very territorial if they're not spayed, and they will vigorously defend that territory. Nature is telling them that if they're going to have a litter of puppies, they'd better stake out some territory to keep those puppies safe. This territory might be just about anything, and you suddenly find that you're banished from certain places in your own home.

Even if a female dog isn't bred she may enter what is called a false or phantom pregnancy. When that happens, she'll pick up a stuffed toy or some other thing in the house in order to have something to mother. If it ends up being your child's Barbie doll, watch out. Your little girl innocently reaches down to get her toy and the dog's right there in an instant, saying, "I don't think so! That's my baby you're grabbing."

The hormonal messages that are sent to dogs, both male and female, are very strong. They have to be. They must override everything else in order to ensure that the species survives. But, because these messages are so strong, they drive your dog to do things you don't approve of.

With your female, you'll need to watch her constantly during her approximately 21 days of estrus twice a year. You won't be able to put her in a fenced yard and expect her to stay there, unsupervised, during her seasons. Just like the unneutered male, she's going to be doing everything she possibly can to get out and answer nature's call. It will only take a brief rendezvous with one of the neighborhood dogs to answer that call. Once that happens, you've got to deal with the consequences—a litter of puppies that you're likely not going to want. What's going to happen to them? If you think they'll find good homes, stop in at your local shelter. There aren't enough homes for them all, and each one that does find a home is taking away the potential adoption of a dog already on death row.

While we're talking about things that we *don't* do with our dogs that encourage or create unwanted behavior in them, we should touch on the idea of what happens when you don't train your dog. This may sound a bit odd. Who wouldn't want their dog trained for house manners and general obedience?

It may seem strange, but many owners of beauty contestant dogs, that is, show dogs, don't want to have their dogs trained. This is a bit of a sore spot among many who show their dogs in competition for their looks and their dog's adherence to AKC standards. Some think that training their dogs is the best way of showing not only their physical beauty, but also their temperament and what the dogs are capable of besides looking good. Others feel that it's not a good idea for their beauty contestants because you'll take the fire out of them—the spirit, the pizzazz, the showmanship.

Does it ruin them? In the conformation ring a dog is required to do what's called a stack. That means he has to stand exactly as you placed him while the judge examines him. He has to move on a leash according to the rules of the competition. The interesting thing about this is that show-dog owners don't see preparation for these things as training. Instead, they see it as something they have to do for ring competitions. It is training, and any other sort of training involves the same things their dogs go through for ring competition. The training they do with their dogs in no way diminishes their pizzazz. If it did, no one would win any competitions with a dog that obediently stacked or walked correctly on his leash.

Throughout this book we've talked about the problems that arise from failing to train your dog, so that doesn't need to be re-emphasized here. However, teaching your dog basic obedience commands, whether or not he's a show dog, and using them in everyday life can often make the difference in having an enjoyable companion or a dog that's barely tolerable to be around.

We don't know how other people interact with their show dogs, but ours are a part of the family, and that means we want to have obedient, happy dogs as family members. Their extensive training has never ruined them for the show ring, and we're all a lot happier when we're together outside the ring, which, after all, is most of the time. It's important that you understand that training your dog does not take the pizzazz or spirit out of him—it's the method of training that can cause you problems. If you use the right method, you should only enhance your dog's personality.

Along the same lines as failing to train your dog for good behavior is your dog being unintentionally trained for unwanted behavior. This happens when your dog is inadvertently rewarded by you or someone else for his unwanted behavior. This can happen in unusual ways. For example, where in the world did your dog learn to hate paper carriers? You've had your dog since he was a puppy, and as far as you know, he's never had any sort of interaction with paper carriers, let alone one that would make him want to tear them limb-from-limb. What has happened is that your dog has been unintentionally trained by the paper carrier himself.

Every day, while you're at work, the paper carrier arrives and comes up the walkway to your door. Whenever he does so, your dog flies to the window, barking madly at him. After he puts the paper on the front porch, the paper carrier walks away to continue his rounds. "Yes," your dog is thinking, "I showed him!" Day in and day out, week after week, the paper carrier is training your dog. Your dog is learning that paper carriers are always up to no good, because they're coming onto the pack's turf and then running away when he barks at them. In fact, *every time* he barks at them, they run away; he's rewarded for his behavior because they respond in a satisfying way: they leave when he tells them he wants them to leave. In a short amount of time, your dog has learned that paper carriers should be distrusted and barked at.

There's a little Pomeranian who lives down the street from us. His fenced yard runs parallel to the street. Any time we drive down the street we see him sitting at the corner of the yard waiting for a car to pass. As soon as we begin to pass him he tears along the fence as fast as he can, barking like mad. Naturally, we drive on to our destination. But, we know perfectly well that he's thinking:"Yes! I showed them." If that little dog ever got out of that yard, he'd lose in a run-in with a car that didn't do what he'd been trained to believe it would do: run away, instead of hitting him.

The old adage, as the twig is bent, so the tree is inclined," is descriptive of what happens when you fail to become the pack leader for your dog, or your kids. Your dog is only going to be a baby for a short time, just a few months. No matter how cute or cuddly he may be, by the time he's nine months old you better have laid the foundation for control and obedience for living with a full-grown, adult dog. If you fail to accept the responsibility of doing so and of being pack leader while he's still a puppy, you're headed for behavior problems of all kinds in just a short while. As a twig, you need to get him straightened out for obedience, because when he gets to be a tree it's going to be a lot harder to do so. What he learns as a puppy is going to influence how he behaves as an adult.

It doesn't matter what kind of dog you have. You don't want negative behavior from either a Poodle or a Great Dane. But, when you start talking about dogs with considerable size and power, like a Rottweiler, you can't afford not to be pack leader and establish control and obedience in him early on in his life. If you fail to be pack leader, your own or someone else's life may become threatened.

Failure to be pack leader will also have unpleasant—maybe even fatal—consequences for your dog. Many owners with powerful dogs who fail to establish their leadership with them find that they have a very large dog who's uncontrollable. When that happens, they get scared and the dog ends up under the needle.

Most of these owners are good people who mean well, but once they become frightened of their dogs, any desire to progress grinds to a halt. You'd better be pack leader for your dog—and your kids—early on, because as they mature they may dominate you.

This kind of pack leadership has to be established regardless of what sort of family structure you have. Your puppy, for example, comes from a single-parent home. Watch a mother dog. She's a single parent and she gets along just fine with her kids because she establishes control over them right from the start and never apologizes about the single parent set-up.

Human single parents often seem to spend time apologizing to their children for having only one parent. They try to compensate by coddling their youngster, making it up to him for not having a normal life. In doing so, they compromise their leadership. They're saying, "I can't be a good leader for you because I'm on my own."

There's no perfect situation for parenting that works the same for everyone. Neither is any particular child-rearing situation always a hardship for the child. Mother dogs do fine with their pups because that's the way it is for them; it's the situation they're in and they simply work within that framework. There's no mother dog imparting to her children how sad she is for them because the father dog isn't around. You have what you have, and that's it. You all have to learn to accept life on its own terms, and as you deal with your children and your dogs, it's your responsibility to equip them to cope with life. Your kids will listen and learn from you no matter what your child-rearing situation is like, if they respect you as the leader.

What about families that have step-parents? That can be a troubling situation. There's always this problem of getting the child to obey the new father or mother: "You're not my *real* dad (mom)!"

If you have a 10-year-old boy with a new step-father, the boy will test the bounds of that new authority figure. For his part, the step-father may be hesitant about being too assertive, for fear it might cause problems with his spouse, the mother of the child. Similarly, he might want to avoid being assertive at all, since his natural inclination is to want the boy to like him.

This is the same thing that goes on among parents of a new dog. It's going to be necessary to make some adjustments so that the new family can still run smoothly. One of these is that both parents have to be leaders, not just one. In the case of the step-father, he's going to have to assert his authority, or things are going to fall apart. With the dog, the same thing may be going on: You don't want to be assertive with him because you want the little guy to like you. In both cases, with the boy and the dog, both parents have to be the leaders, not just one.

You need to agree in advance what methods you're going to use to establish and maintain obedience, and you need to agree on what the rules are. You have to present a unified front for creating and maintaining control, respect, and thus obedience. If one of you is telling the dog to sit before he gets fed, and the other never mentions it, there will be nothing but confusion for the dog because he's going to end up violating someone's rules.

This isn't the dog's fault, but rather the fault of the dog's parents who have failed to clarify the rules and be consistent. Similarly, if the child's mother doesn't want him to do something and the boy runs to the step-father for approval and he gives it because he doesn't want the kid to not like him, mom's authority just flew out the window.

We have a standard reaction to parents who disagree on parenting styles: you're both wrong. When parents fail to agree, they create confusion and disharmony in the pack. The art of compromise means you both win a little and lose a little. When you agree, the big winners are your kids who see adults as having their best interests at heart. This is true whether those kids have two legs or four.

Part of maintaining your leadership role is not giving it away. Many people get a puppy for their child to raise. This is just about the worst thing you could do for your dog. You can get a puppy for the family, but he should always be mom's or dad's dog. That means that when the dog needs something, you can say: "This is my dog, and this is what he needs."

When you give a child a dog, you've given him the authority to control the dog's upbringing before he has either the maturity or the emotional tools to do it right. In addition, many children don't want the responsibility of caring for and raising a dog who has many needs. The dog suffers as a consequence. While it's an extreme case, the following still serves to illustrate the need for you to be the dog's leader, not your child.

We evaluated a situation in which a woman who had a child with Attention Deficit Disorder Syndrome (ADDS) and a Black Labrador. To say that the child was willful would be an understatement. ADDS often results in hyperactivity, and this particular child exhibited many of the more negative symptoms of this. The well-intentioned mother felt that getting the boy a puppy would be a good educational tool, and that it would teach him both responsibility and much-needed patience.

The six-year-old boy suddenly had to get up during the evaluation to take his puppy outside to relieve himself. He was also responsible for feeding the puppy, but it was clear he didn't want these responsibilities. On top of that, he actually hated the dog. Sadly, the dog served as the object of the boy's frustrations.

On her first visit to the Academy, we noticed that the puppy didn't seem to be feeling very well, and we said so. The woman said "I'm not sure if he ate any of the tacks." The boy had actually fed tacks to the puppy. We got him to the vet as fast as we could and, sure enough, the X-rays showed that the puppy had in fact eaten two or three tacks. Luckily, the vet was able to remove the tacks before they tore the little guy to pieces.

This turned out to be a complicated case because of the particular family dynamics involved. However, the woman was attached to the puppy and didn't want to give him up. The first thing that had to happen if they were going to keep the dog is that the woman had to reclaim responsibility for her dog. She had to be pack leader because no one else was equipped to be.

Behaviors of all kinds can emerge in your dog for many different reasons. Sometimes, you're the cause of these negative influences even if you don't realize it. If you misunderstand what sort of dog you're bringing home to become a family member, or if you fail to interact with your dog in ways that reinforce positive behavior, you can create an environment in which your dog learns unwanted behavior.

Sometimes it takes a professional to understand why these problems emerge in a dog, because it's not always clear at first what might have sparked that particular behavior. That's why you're reading this book. It's tough to be a canine behavioralist yourself, but getting some insight into the variety of things that can influence your dog's behavior may give you some insight as to how to go about addressing some of those issues.

Chapter 8
Physiology & Behavior

Throughout this third section of the book, we've been trying to drive home the idea that your dog's behavior is dependent on a wide variety of influences. Some of these have to do with pack matters because they involve pack dynamics in your home. Other influences on your dog's behavior are sometimes unwittingly created by misunderstanding your dog's temperament or by failing to do certain things with him. These have to do with your dog's environment and how you and he interact within thatenvironment. But, matters that are going on inside your dog, not just surroundings, can also have an impact on his behavior.

Diet and Behavioral Shifts

Most people understand that when you're affected physically, you're affected emotionally as well. You realize that when you have the flu, you aren't in the perkiest of moods. That's why it seems strange that people don't consider how diet affects them emotionally. After all, diet is one of the most basic and fundamental features of human physiology. You would think that more people would make the connection between diet and how they feel. The truth is that diet is significant in influencing your feelings and subsequently behavior—the same is true with your dog.

There are too many variables to offer you a troubleshooting guide for diet and canine behavior, and dogs do not react in any predictable way to a particular diet. All we're trying to say is that your dog's unwanted behavior may be diet related.

For example, some dogs are allergic to certain foods: grains, vegetables, meats or dairy products. You don't need to be a veterinarian or a nutritional expert to understand that if your dog isn't feeling well because of an allergic reaction to food, he isn't going to exhibit his best behavior.

One of our trainers has found that her dog doesn't seem to do well after eating lamb. For about an hour after eating, this normally passive dog would scratch his muzzle and act very disagreeable toward anyone who got too close to him. She altered his diet and never saw that behavior again. The only change in his diet was the absence of lamb. This was a rather subtle change in a dog's behavior, but other physiological clues, like a dull coat or excessive shedding or skin irritations, may indicate something in his diet.

Shortly after the episode with our trainer's dog, we had a dog come in for an evaluation who committed random acts of aggression. Her behavior patterns didn't seem to fit the dog's breed, training and overall profile. Recalling the earlier case of diet-related aggressiveness, we suggested to the owners that they have their dog tested for allergies. Sure enough, their dog was allergic to the meat products in her regular food.

If you're on a constant diet of nutritionally poor food, it's going to affect you in some way. You may not have as much energy, you may find yourself depressed over nothing at all, and you're likely going to be more susceptible to illness. The same thing goes for your dog. Some of the less expensive dog foods are about as nutritional as sawdust. They make your dog feel full and they may taste great so he always eats his meals with relish. However, they may not be nutritional, and as a result, diet-related negative behaviors may emerge.

Interestingly, some dogs develop what is called food anxiety because they are eating highly nutritional foods available in many pet food stores. These foods are so nutritional that your dog doesn't need as much of them. Although they may be getting enough nutrition, some dogs feel unsatisfied because they're not eating enough bulk to feel full. They may become anxious around mealtimes, hounding you for more food after they've already eaten. Check your dog's nutritional needs with either a veterinarian or a knowledgeable source at a good feed store.

We've heard of several instances of dogs becoming physically disturbed before mealtimes. One person told us that their Rottweiler became weak-kneed and wobbly before feeding, and had a very disagreeable temper until after he had eaten. Similar cases that we've read about seem to suggest that this behavior is not simply a matter of being hungry, but something related to a dog's diet.

The bottom line is, diet matters. When people see sudden aggressive behavior in their dogs they're inclined to panic. Allergic reactions to diet are so common, it's one of the first things that should be considered when you see sudden behavioral shifts in your dog. Diet affects your dog physically, and may affect him emotionally and behaviorally. Do your dog and yourself a big favor by learning what's best for him. Seek out competent advice from either a veterinarian or a specialist.

Physical Ailments and your Dog's Behavior

As with diet, anything that is a physical influence on your dog may also influence his behavior. Your dog's overall health and physical well-being are of great importance to his behavior. We are constantly amazed when clients come in and fill out the initial registration form that includes questions about their dog's general health, and even though a dog may be tearing his skin off because of fleas or shuffling along on deformed legs, clients generally write down *good*. Some people don't seem to understand how important it is to know how their dogs act when healthy. How else can they know if their dogs aren't feeling well and begin to act uncharacteristically?

First, you need to know what is a healthy dog? A healthy dog should quite literally have bright eyes and a good coat. By a good coat, we mean one that is consistent with his breed standard. For example, good means a silky, glossy, shiny coat for many long-haired breeds. But, other breeds should have a stiff, wiry coat. Your dog should be able to walk loosely and freely within his conformational constraints— that is, a Basset Hound and a Brittany Spaniel will have very different styles of movement, each of which is normal for the respective breed. There should be no unusual amounts of mucus at the corners of his eyes, and his teeth should be strong and white. For a great many breeds, certain ailments and physical defects are rather common. For example, German Shepherds often suffer from hip dysplasia, and certain other breeds are susceptible to poor eyesight. You should talk to a professional about what these breed-related ailments are so you can be a better judge of your dog's overall health.

Earaches

Just like a person who suffers from constant ear pain, a dog with chronically bad ears is going to be cranky much of the time. We were called as witnesses in a recent court case involving a dog who had bad ears. The trial involved a Springer Spaniel who had bitten a child.

We spent three days in court hearing testimony against and providing testimony for the dog based on our positions as canine behaviorists. The prosecution had brought in a dog behaviorist who spoke against the Springer, citing extensive research done on aggressive Springers who have been known to manifest "Springer Rage." There is a belief that this is a genetic predisposition in some Springers, usually from a particular bloodline, which stemmed from selective breeding that resulted in some nasty side effects.

During the trial, we warned against this generalizing of Springer Spaniels as a breed, arguing that doing so was like diagnosing a headache for someone whose family had a history of migraines. That particular individual might be suffering from something like sinus trouble that had nothing to do with the family's predisposition to migraine headaches.

Whether it's a court trial or not, behaviorists should look at all aspects of a particular case instead of just saying: "Yeah, it bit a child because it was a Springer." In this particular case, the circumstances didn't fit the scenario for Springer Rage. In the end, the dog was acquitted because the defense was able to prove that the child who was bitten had actually provoked the attack. He had teased the dog repeatedly, but had done so on this occasion when the dog had had a bad earache. Because of the pain, the dog essentially said: "That's it. I can't take this from you anymore," and bit the child. This was not a case of Springer Rage, just a bad earache.

Certain breeds with drooping ears deserve special comment here because such dogs are much more susceptible to ear infection than dogs whose ears are short or upright. Your dog cannot take care of this particular aspect of personal hygiene himself. Dogs are lousy with swabs, anyway. No matter what breed of dog you have, keep his ears clean at all times. If you've got a Basset Hound or a dog with similarly drooping ears, keep close watch on them.

Vaginitis and Bladder Infections

Whenever you're confronted by a dog with a behavioral problem, look first at the simple things. It's like your car. If it's not running right, you're better off changing your filters or spark plugs before you decide to drop a new engine in it. You might be surprised. Some dogs that are exhibiting behavioral problems may be merely suffering from common, temporary canine ailments.

For example, younger female dogs are prone to vaginitis, which in turn can lead to more serious bladder infections if not treated. We have folks coming into the Academy complaining that their dogs have suddenly started urinating all over the house. In many instances, the dog has simply developed a bladder infection and has to urinate of-

Doc...I've got this pain...

ten. The infection puts pressure on the bladder causing the dog to feel the need to urinate much more often than she normally would. As a result, the dog can't hold it until her normally scheduled outings for release. Once the infection clears up, this behavior ends.

Thyroid Conditions

As with people, medical ailments involve a wide variety of problems. If you're not feeling right, it's not always something obvious that's affecting you. Even if it's not serious, the obvious ailments aren't always the culprits. And, as so often happens when you're not feeling right, the obvious problems are only symptoms of something else going on. This is true of your dog as well. For example, your dog may have chronic ear infections, but that in itself may only be a symptom of something else going on, like a thyroid condition.

The thyroid gland secretes a hormone that can influence behavior. This is true of both dogs and people. If a dog becomes low thyroid—his thyroid gland is not producing normal amounts of its particular hormone—then his behavior may change radically. Dogs that are low thyroid, which is considerably more common than dogs who are high thyroid, don't seem to handle stress well. They become agitated easily, or are frightened by things that should not appear threatening to them.

This reaction to stress may cause the dog to behave in a way that you might consider aggressive behavior. However, the truth may be that he is biting or snapping at everyone and everything more out of fear than true aggression.

Other dogs become frantic when they are low thyroid. We've had dogs like this at the Academy who were nearly impossible to train because of the difficulty in breaking through their panic. When a dog is under so much stress that he can't pay attention, you can't train him.

While thyroid conditions in dogs are not particularly rare, you shouldn't jump to conclusions about what's causing a sudden behavioral shift in your dog. For one thing, if your dog is going through a Fear Imprint Stage, it's normal for him to react strangely to what would otherwise be a nonstressful situation. If you are able to eliminate other causes for your dog's strange behavior, it is possible to have a thyroid test done to determine if his hormonal status is normal or not.

Injuries

Dogs can become aggressive as a result of an injury. We've seen a number of dogs who had been injured that continued to find being handled an unpleasant experience, even after they had returned to health. It's as if they have trained themselves to react protectively to a particular area of their bodies, even though the actual pain has long since ceased to bother them. When someone reaches to pet them, they automatically tense. If a dog gets too tense, his contracted muscles may bring the old pain back, and thus reinforce his belief that being touched is not a good thing.

Conclusion

It's impossible to list all the breed-related ailments that exist. They may include respiratory problems, bone cancers, eyelid surgeries, skin problems, allergies, brittle bones, slipping kneecaps and poor eyesight, to name a few. In addition, the general life expectancy of your breed of dog should be taken into consideration, as this will give you some sense of the number of trips to the vet you can expect to make during your dog's lifetime.

Even though it's impossible to provide a detailed list of these potential problems, a couple of examples will give you some idea of the range of things you should check regarding any breed of dog you may choose. For example, some breeds, like Chow Chows, Shar-Peis and Bulldogs, are prone to lower eyelids that are inclined to roll inward. This causes irritated eyelashes and possible eye injuries. One-time surgery doesn't always fix the problem, either.

We've seen Bulldogs undergo this expensive procedure several times before reaching two years of age. As another example, Portuguese Water Dogs have been known to have a disease of the cells called Storage Disease. Because of the similarity of this malady to one suffered in Jewish bloodlines, the Jewish community has funded research to develop early tests that have eradicated the disease from all but a few dogs. Unfortunately, most breed-related ailments do not have such funding working to solve them.

Check the medical history for the breed you're about to bring home. This precaution may help to anticipate the onset of some ailment. If you have some sense of the kinds of medical ailments your dog is susceptible to, either general maladies or breed-related ones, you may be able to anticipate potential behavioral changes in your dog.

PART IV
THE JOYS OF PARENTING

Chapter 9
Are You Ready For This?

Throughout this book, we've talked about parenting your dog as opposed to training him or just owning him. The reason parenting is a more accurate term to describe the relationship between you and your dog is that training doesn't depict a complete mental picture of everything involved in that relationship. Nor does training suggest the kind of constancy that's necessary for true, life-long obedience—the kind of obedience that you should expect in any situation. The notion of parenting is much more inclusive of what's going on between you and your dog. For one thing, your dog really is a family member, much as your children are family members. Parenting is also more suggestive of the similarities involved in creating and maintaining obedience in your children *and* your dogs.

Almost any consideration that can be applied to your kids can be applied to your dog, and probably should be in most cases. Consider the similarities between deciding to have children and deciding to get a dog. When you decide to have children, you may wonder if you have a clear sense of what you're getting into. Having a baby is a big decision, but, sometimes you don't realize just how big a decision it really is until the baby arrives. Oh, sure, you've been dashing around for months getting furniture to refurbish the spare bedroom into a baby's room, and you've bought clothes and checked into getting the proper foods and formulas.

You're all set. Then the baby arrives. After a while, you notice that you have almost no social life. It's not easy packing up the baby for a night out on the town, and suddenly a quiet night of television is the best you can manage. And boy, that little baby needs to be looked after constantly.

You had no idea that this would be such an utterly full-time undertaking. There's so much involved in having a baby, but it seems like there's even more involved in caring for one. Sometimes you wonder if new parents understood all this when they started planning for their baby.

There's a great deal involved with getting a dog, too, that many people don't think about. You saw that coming, didn't you? Well, it's true. You might go out and buy a puppy or a dog, pick up a bag of grocery store food and a couple of durable bowls and figure that's it. If you're thoughtful, you might even pick up a leash, a collar, and maybe a doggie toy or two. You're all set, right? Well, some folks know better, but for those of you out there who are thinking about getting your first dog, let's see.

Tools of the Trade

People often fail to give much thought to the tools needed to raise a healthy, happy dog. You might go out and spend a small fortune purchasing a dog, but not consider the costs of what's involved in raising him. To give you a better idea of what *is* involved, let's take a quick look at the material items your dog will need:

COLLAR. The first thing your dog needs is a collar. If for nothing else, your dog needs a collar so you can have something to attach his identification information to. Make sure your dog has proper identification tags on him at all times. If he gets lost, this may make all the difference in getting him back. There are all kinds of collars, not just in terms of looks or style, but also in terms of function. Your dog needs at least two collars. One of these will be a nonslip or buckle collar, one that won't allow him to choke. For a little puppy, cat collars work well because a small segment of the collar is an elastic strip that allows the puppy to pull it off over his head if he snags it on something. When he's older, though, get him a nonslip, buckle collar.

You'll also need a training collar—a check-chain collar. These are preferred by most professionals to aid in your dog's training. Because the chain of the collar slides through one of its rings, the dog can't back his head out of it like he can with a nylon or a leather buckle collar. This is very useful when training a dog who would rather not be trained, and who tries to make a quick getaway by slipping out of his buckle collar. With one of those, you may find yourself during a training session holding onto a leash with nothing but the collar attached to it.

Dogs who are impervious to pain, particularly willful or just plain inattentive may require a more assertive correction. For these, you may wish to purchase what is called a pinch collar. These collars look more ominous than they really are. They consist of a loop of blunt prongs that, when used to give a correction, cause the loop to collapse, pinching the dog's skin. They do not—repeat, do not—puncture the dog's skin. Unlike check-chains, these collars have a fail-safe loop that prevents the collar from becoming too tight. These collars may be quite shocking to a dog who has never experienced an ounce of noticeable discomfort in his life. That's the whole idea—to get the attention of a dog who can't pay attention any other way. These collars may serve as an equalizer when the trainer is very small and the dog is very large, or the handler has some physical problem that may cause difficulty controlling even a small dog. It's like having power steering on a big truck. If you are considering a pinch collar, check with a professional so he can confirm that it's the right choice for your situation. You should also receive instructions on how to fit the collar properly. A poorly fitted collar can cause the dog unneccessary discomfort. The pet equipment industry is very active in producing new training equipment. There are many types of collars created to help solve specific problems, but it is best to check with a professional for advice.

LEASH. You're also going to need a good leash. While your dog is still a puppy, you can get away with a light-weight, inexpensive one. As he gets older, though, invest in a good quality leather leash that is comfortable to your hand. If the leash is comfortable and easy to hold, you're less likely to get frustrated and short-tempered when handing your dog; it'll give you more leverage and you won't feel as if you've got to pull with all your might to administer a correction. Also, if you've got a large or even medium-sized dog and you're using a light-weight nylon leash, you're in for a nasty surprise when he suddenly pulls hard against you. You can almost smell your skin burning as that nylon slashes through your grip.

One of the most overlooked aspects of selecting a good leash is the snap or lock that attaches the leash to the collar. Be sure to investigate the size of the snap on a given leash for size, weight and strength of the snap. If you get a poor leash, that snap is the weakest link in your control over your dog. Get a leash with a snap that's appropriate to the size and strength of your dog, but don't get one that's so big that it hurts him if it bumps against him.

Remember that when you're walking your dog that snap is right up there around your dog's eye. You don't want a leash with a snap that's going to smack him in the face. On the other hand, if you've got a Rottweiler puppy you don't want a Toy Poodle-sized snap because it's not going to hold him. If your dog learns that pulling hard enough will break the snap, he learns to challenge both you and your equipment.

No matter where you live, a leash is an important piece of equipment. Don't be fooled into thinking you can get away without one just because you live in a rural area where you don't have to worry about traffic. You don't have to be out in the country to lose your dog, either. Here comes a squirrel and here comes a truck. You're only three feet away from your dog when he bolts after the squirrel and into the street. You can't run as fast as your dog, so the squirrel gets across the street, but you can't get to your dog and he doesn't make it. Much better to ensure constant control with a leash on your dog, no matter where you are. Even if you've got good voice control over your dog, you won't have that same kind of control over the other guy's dog.

You also need a leash for training. A training leash can be a signal to your dog that school is in session. There comes a time in every puppy's life when it's appropriate for him to start dragging a leash around while you're home to supervise. This helps train you, too. It teaches you to keep your hands off your dog. If your puppy jumps on you and you're training him not to, but you don't have a leash on him, you have to put your hands on him to put him down or push him away. For him, though, that's a free massage; he's getting rewarded for behavior you're trying to stop because he likes to have your hands on him. But, if the leash is on the puppy, then you can pick up the end as needed when you give a command. For his jumping up on you or trying to dash through a door without permission, that trailing leash can be stepped on so that he administers a self-correction.

IDENTIFICATION. Returning to the need for identification for your dog, the most likely time for him to run away and get lost is soon after he's come into your home. He doesn't know his way around, and if he gets away from you it's going to be nearly impossible for him to find his way back. All kinds of ID tags are available, and it's also possible to have your dog tattooed or fitted with a computer-chip insert that can be read by shelters in your area. Whatever kind of ID you opt for, do it fast. If you don't have proper ID while you're seeking out which kind to get for him, or if there's a short wait while you're getting your tag back from an engraver, write down all the relevant information on a sheet of paper, wrap it around your dog's collar, wrap that with plastic wrap, and tape it on. Now you've got short-term wind and water-proof ID on him until you can get something permanent. If he has a nylon collar, take a pen and write the information on the collar itself.

Joys of Parenting

CRATE. A dog crate is a great investment, and particularly important for a puppy. A crate is the safest way of transporting him, but it's got a wide variety of uses for your dog. Dog crates are often misunderstood. You might think it's a cage or a little prison. To your dog, however, it's a bedroom, a safe place to hide out when there's too much activity going on, and it's his own little piece of real estate right there in the house. A crate is a place of sanctuary for your dog; it's a place where he can go for some peace and quiet, especially when there are children in the family.

A crate should never be an instrument of punishment. It shouldn't be something you angrily consign your dog to when you find him chewing on your new pair of shoes. If you want him out of the way or stop some mischief, fine, but take him to his crate and quietly close the door. Don't toss him in there, telling him what a bad dog he is for chewing your shoes.

The crate should be a positive thing, and for most dogs it is. Be clear about this when your puppy is in his crate. Leave him alone when he's there, so that he can understand that this is a place of refuge for peace. If you can get your puppy used to this idea, he'll appreciate the fact that, when things get hectic and he gets put in his crate, you're running interference for him so he doesn't have to put up with bother. If there are little kids in the house, he may appreciate this time on his own, and when you put him in his crate it takes pressure off him for having to look after and defend himself from little grabbing hands.

Once he goes into his crate, don't allow a child to pull him out. That's a recipe for disaster. Your puppy may defend his piece of real estate. If the child reaches in and the puppy snaps at him and the child screams and runs away, the puppy's thinking, "Ha! Gotcha." Just like that, you have a dog who's learning that biting will help him get what he wants, in this case just to be left alone for a while.

Don't leave food and water in there with him. You might think you're doing your puppy a favor when you leave him confined with food and water, but you're not. He's going to need to relieve himself after a while if he eats or drinks, and if you're not around to let him out, it's going to be torture for him. He certainly doesn't want to relieve himself in his sleeping area, but you may force him to.

A crate is an important piece of equipment during the housetraining period with your puppy, but that training is usually completed relatively early on. The real reason you want a crate is to help avoid your puppy's potentially destructive behavior. He's going to go through a real need-to-chew-something phase that will last quite a while. At night when you're asleep and can't supervise him, he may be tempted to wander around looking for something to chew. This is when you discover that your puppy has taken a real liking to your imported handbag or your best pair of gloves.

You should probably keep your puppy in his crate at night for at least his first year. After that, you'll have to decide if his chewing days are over enough for him to be loose in the house at night. If you don't have a crate and feel like you can't get one anytime soon, don't try using an open-topped box as an alternative. The open top will make him feel vulnerable. If you must, try putting the box on its side, with the opening facing outward. At least that will be more like a den to him. Don't get a puppy without having the means to contain him, which is something you will definitely need to do for a time.

Don't resort to having him crated constantly. That's when the crate really does become a prison. He can't be shut in the crate all the time, because he can't move around enough in there to stretch his legs very well, let alone get a bit of exercise. Don't resort to tying the puppy to something because your puppy may learn to chew through leashes. And, once he's loose, the trouble really starts.

You may think you can lock the dog in a room when you're gone, but the puppy is likely to get traumatized in your absence. Being chained up for long periods of time isn't a good option either: your dog's freedom of movement is restricted and it frustrates him, making him agitated and unhappy.

There's no reason to do these things because exercise pens are available. Exercise pens are essentially collapsible wire boxes. They fold down into a flat stack of wire sides, and so are completely transportable and easily stored when you're not using them. They come in a variety of sizes. If you've got a little Shih Tzu who is never going to get very big, you can get away with an ex-pen that's only got 24-inch-high panels. If you've got larger or more active dogs, you want something bigger. If your dog is the active type, attach the ex-pen to a tree or something sturdy so it can't be tipped over. You can use duct tape to secure an ex-pen to a linoleum floor. You can even combine two or more ex-pens to make a portable rambler for your dog.

Some apartment dwellers use exercise pens out on the small grassy areas that surround their apartment building. They move them around every day or two so the grass won't be damaged and so their dog has a new location to relieve himself on a regular basis. Perhaps you've already raised three or four dogs without owning either a crate or an exercise pen, but keep in mind that your new dog is going to have an entirely different personality from your previous dogs. Young dogs are much like toddlers—some of them have low curiosity levels and some of them are highly tactile, wanting to touch, feel and taste everything within their reach. Some dogs are going to be mellow when you're raising them, and others are going to be everywhere and into everything.

We see people in at the Academy who say: "We tried to barricade the puppy in the kitchen, but he kept getting out." And, once the little rascal got out, he ruined their clothing, carpet, cupboards and curtains. They kept trying to confine him, using all kinds of barriers, but his desire to get out was stronger than their inventiveness. The problem could have been avoided if they had had an exercise pen in their kitchen. With a crate inside the pen, their dog could have had a great little set-up, and the owners wouldn't have been shopping for new carpet.

RUG. You want to get your dog a decent rug, too. Bony dogs in particular need a place where they can comfortably lay their unpadded bodies. It's difficult for them to rest comfortably without something like a rug to lay on. The best sort of rug you can get is one that's rubber-backed and washable. The reason you want a washable rug should be obvious, but you want a rubber-backed one so that if it's put down on a slippery surface it won't go sliding all over the place, and neither will you when you walk across it.

You might want to use carpet samples as dog rugs and throw them away. But, even if your dog has a body configuration or coat that makes you wonder if he's even got bones at all under all that, you still want a rug. Teaching your dog to go to his rug, and to stay there for short periods of time can be really useful. When you come in from that walk in the rain, you can have him go to his rug for awhile until he dries off. His rug can also be a pleasant spot from which to observe company, while staying out of harm's way. It's also a nice spot for him because you can still have him with you, but he won't annoy your company, and he'll be removed somewhat from annoying guests as well.

Get a rug that will be your dog's rug at all times. Don't just pull one out of the closet when you want one for a particular situation. Get him one he can call his own. It'll be easier to train him to go to his rug and stay put if he feels like the rug is his. Take your rug along when you go visiting. As soon as you put it down, your dog has his own little spot of familiar ground in unfamiliar surroundings. Both your dog and your friends will appreciate his ability to lie down comfortably and out of the way.

GROOMING TOOLS. Regardless of breed, you're going to need grooming tools to keep up with his personal hygiene. Unlike cats, dogs aren't nearly so inclined to keep themselves clean and, like a cat, there are some things they simply cannot do for themselves. It doesn't matter if you've got a long- or short-haired dog, you need some grooming equipment. The breed of dog you have will determine much of what you will buy to take care of his coat. Combs and brushes are available in great variety, each one reflecting the variety of needs among many breeds and coat types. You should evaluate your dog's coat needs so you can make proper choices about which combs and brushes to have on hand. Some dogs with very long coats may need to have feces removed from their hind quarters on a frequent basis because their coats are in the way. Also, many dogs with heavy or long coats have several layers of fur, an outer coat and an undercoat. As a result, you may need several different kinds of combs and brushes to accommodate his needs.

We recommend having both a *rake* brush—one with long, widely separated teeth that can untangle that undercoat—and something like a *slicker* brush that can be used to smooth and untangle his outer coat. This brush has tightly packed, thin teeth on a flat surface. It's great for getting his outer coat smoothed out.

Some dogs also shed more than others, and with these breeds you'll want to keep up with their grooming. German Shepherds, Malamutes and Huskies will drive you mad with their shedding if you don't keep on top of their grooming needs. A *ZoomGroomr* can be a good addition to your grooming tools if you have a "shedder." This is a soft, rubbery grooming tool that is neither a brush nor a comb. It's a flat, hand-sized piece of rubber with numerous soft plastic cones attached. You rub it through your dog's fur to remove loose hair. Many short-coated breeds just love these things because it's like being massaged.

In addition, you may also want to purchase what's called a *stripper*, which is a loop of metal teeth, much like a saw blade bent into a loop, with a handle attached. These are great for stripping loose hair from shorter-haired breeds like German Shepherds that shed a lot. Whatever coat your dog has, grooming is more important than just maintaining his looks. Grooming is part of personal hygiene and thus a part of your dog's overall health. Dirt or debris that gets stuck in his coat near his ears may cause ear infections.

When you're grooming your dog, be sure you don't just slide over the surface of his coat. Always work your fingers down through his fur and onto his skin. Matting in his undercoat will cause him real discomfort because it pulls. If mats go unattended, they can actually pull the skin so tight that it limits the blood supply to the affected area. When the matting is finally removed, the resulting rush of blood to that area can cause a painful internal bruise. Severe matting in a neglected dog can even restrict his movement to the point where his musculature begins to change; one set of muscles will deteriorate while another develops in compensation. Remember then that grooming is important, not just for your dog's looks, but for his overall health.

You need toenail clippers made especially for canine use. We don't recommend any particular style or brand; just get some that both you and your dog are comfortable with. Your dog's toenails should never touch the ground while he is standing. If they do, his toes will be forced to one side or the other, possibly resulting in sprung tendons, leg and hip problems or back pain because your dog will need to compensate for his misguided toes in the way he walks.

Be sure that your dog's first manicure is free of any discomfort. You want him to grow up thinking that this is just a common occurrence. If you clip them too deeply, the quick will likely bleed, but don't be alarmed, you've just tapped into some heavy-duty capillaries. He's in no danger of bleeding to death, but you will want to stop the flow. *Quick-Stop* is a product designed to do just that, but you can apply cornstarch or wheat flour to the affected nail to stop the bleeding.

Keep your clippers sharp. If you have dull clippers you have to apply more pressure to get the job done. Your dog may object to all that squeezing on a sensitive area. Trimming your dog's nails can sometimes become an issue, particularly if you've never learned to do it the right way and you inadvertently cause him pain the first time you try to trim his nails. If you get nervous about doing your dog's nails, he's going to get nervous, too. And if he's jerking his legs while you're trying to work on his nails, you're likely going to cut the quick, reinforcing the idea that this is not a very pleasant procedure. Then the chore just gets harder and harder to perform.

There's no reason this should be a traumatic experience for either of you. You can prevent this from becoming an ordeal by following a few basic guidelines. If you get a puppy, you should start handling his toenails long before trimming them is necessary. That way he's already accustomed to the sensation when it comes time for his first pedicure. If you're unsure about the way to do it, take your dog to a groomer so that his first experience is a painless one, and also so you can observe how it's done. Look at the toenail from the bottom. You can see the area at the end that looks much like your own fingernails. You want to trim the outer portion of the nail while avoiding cutting into the quick, which is noticeable from its difference in coloration.

Even with dogs who have dark nails, you should be able to see which portion is the quick at the base of each nail. Start trimming your puppy's nails by just barely trimming the tips, but do it routinely. This will help make the process easier in the end. You want to start trimming your dog's nails early on in his life, because if they're allowed to grow too long, the quick gets longer. That means you'll have a harder time getting his nails to the proper size because trimming them will almost inevitably require *quicking* them.

If you have a dog that violently objects to having his nails trimmed, you want to progress in increments. Start out with a gentle massaging of the feet and legs, rubbing his toes and getting him accustomed to the idea that you can handle these areas without discomfort to him. Talk to him while you're doing this, using a calm, quiet voice. Next, touch his nails with the clippers, but don't clip them yet. You just want your dog to see what it feels like. Let your dog hear the clippers clip a few times. Continue to massage his feet gently. When you think your dog is comfortable with all this, try clipping a nail or two, but only the tip, even if you have to leave them a bit long to start with. Again, make sure your clippers are sharp before you begin, because he will object to the squeezing if not the trimming itself.

Don't allow your dog to have his mouth on you in any way during this process. He is not in control of any part of the procedure, and the fact that he may fuss at you is no reason to give up. If you give up, he wins. You just trained him that he can get what he wants if he just fusses enough. If all this doesn't work for you, you may want to have a professional do this for you on a regular basis. Some breeds simply do not like having their nails trimmed, particularly their more sensitive front ones. Trimming your dog's nails can sometimes change an otherwise mellow dog into one who comes unglued when he sees you pull out the clippers.

TOYS. Toys should also be on the list of basic needs for your dog. Toys for your dog, like toys for your kids, are necessary for staving off boredom and burning off energy. Some toys are mentally stimulating and require concentration, and it's a good idea to exercise both your dog's muscles and his mental playfulness. But, as with your other kids, you should choose your dog's toys with care. Some selections in your dog's playthings may come to haunt you later on. For example, many dogs love to play with flying discs like *Frisbees*. These are great fun for both you and your dog. However, many of these flying discs are made of hard plastic, which can have unpleasant side effects. For one thing, catching a hard plastic disc is hard on your dog's teeth and mouth. In colder temperatures, that little disc is rock-hard and is liable to break one of his teeth if it slams into his mouth. Also, these discs may seem like a plastic food or water bowl to your dog. If he develops a tendency to chew on that *Frisbee* while he's playing catch, he may also want to chew his food bowl to bits when he's bored.

There are better options available for this kind of toy. Manufacturers are now making versions of the flying disc in rip-stop nylon. They soar, and there's no worry about hurting your dog's teeth when he catches one. They're also washable. However, they are susceptible to being chewed, just like the plastic discs, so it's not a good idea to leave them lying around.

Chews can be left lying around all the time, allowing your dog constant access to them, because that's what they're for. There are all kinds of good chew toys on the market these days—*Nylabones*, *Kongs*, *Plaque-Attackers*, and many more. They all serve the same purpose: giving your dog something to chew that satisfies his urge to chew and something that will help keep his teeth clean.

Chewing is a real stress-reliever for some dogs, and it's fun, too. But, chewing is important to your dog for other reasons as well. You might not realize that dogs need to chew until they're a year old. First they go through the teething stage in which they chew on things to help push their teeth up through their gums, and then they need to chew things again after their adult teeth have come in. During this second stage your dog's teeth are set into the jaw, anchored into the bone, by chewing.

As with all toys, however, choose a chew toy that's appropriate for your dog's size and habits. Don't get him one that's so small that he might swallow the darn thing, and don't get him one that's so big that he can't get a good grip on it.

While there are many good chew toys to get your dog, there are also ones that you shouldn't get, particularly ones made of rawhide. Rawhide expands when it gets wet. If your dog bites off and swallows a hunk of rawhide—this is easier than you think because rawhide also gets slimy when it's wet and can slide down his throat—that chunk of leather can expand and block his intestine, killing him. Rawhide products are often imported from nations that use nasty stuff when curing the leather, such as urine and harsh chemicals—things you don't want your dog to ingest. Besides, with all the other great chew products available out there, why mess with something that can be potentially harmful to your dog.

There are other doggy toys you need to evaluate before you buy. The so-called squeaky toys are available in just about any shape and size you can imagine. Be careful when purchasing these, though. Because they are usually made of lightweight rubber or plastic, they're easy to chew to bits in a hurry, and thus much more likely than a chew toy to get swallowed. Evaluate your dog's size and chewing habits, and get what's right for him.

You need to decide in advance how toys are going to be used so you don't inadvertently teach unwanted behavior. Consider carefully if you want your dog to get used to a shoe as a chew toy.

Some toys are more associated with training than they are playtime, so you need to decide how and when your dog has access to them. Bumpers are a case in point. Bumpers, for the most part, are hollow plastic tubes. Some look like giant, hard-plastic hot-dogs. Others are made of canvas for soft-mouthed dogs and for puppies who cannot get a bite on a large tube. Canvas bumpers are desirable for puppies because they don't damage their teeth. Because bumpers float, they make great training tools when training a dog to retrieve. The long knobby tube of the bumper has a hole at the top that allows you to tie a rope to it so you don't lose it in the water during the early stages of training. Or, you can tie a short rope to it for greater throwing leverage. These are excellent training tools. For your younger dog who is reluctant to relinquish his prize, the bumper offers an object that can be easily slid from his mouth. For the beginning retriever, a tennis ball can be entirely contained within his mouth, so it's not as easy to get away from him.

When you get a bumper, decide what it's going to be used for. Dogs love to chew on these just as much as anything else, so if you get it for training purposes, put it away immediately after training. "Absence makes the heart grow fonder," so if your dog is fond of his bumper but can only have it during training, this can increase his desire to go after it.

Similarly, don't use your dog's chew toys as training tools. The two different uses for a single object will only confuse him. After all, with his chew toy his natural inclination is not to retrieve it, but rather to lie down and chew on it. Decide in advance what a given toy is going to be used for, and how and when your dog will have access to it.

That's enough to get you started. If you're thinking about getting a dog, keep in mind all the things that go along with having one. Like a child, your dog has needs beyond food and shelter, and it's helpful to have realistic expectations for what these needs are and what they're going to cost you. Medical bills, food, obedience classes, grooming tools and toys can add up, but, before you call up the bank for an extension on your credit, take some time to make a list of the things you need for a dog and then call around to your local pet and feed stores.Don't forget that time is an important consideration also because the time needed to raise a puppy properly can really add up.

Chances are that the things you need to raise a happy, healthy dog won't break the bank after all. Even though this chapter asks the question, are you ready for this, the expected response is, "Yes, I'm ready." When you plan to have kids it's a lot more realistic to assume that you can't anticipate everything that raising them will involve, but you have your children anyway. The joy of having them and the love and satisfaction that go into raising them far outweigh any belated realizations regarding needs. You find a way. The same is true with your dog. If you really want one and you really want him to be happy and healthy, you just take care of it, no matter what it takes. We hope this chapter has given you a clearer sense of what *is* involved in raising your dog, so that you'll be able to anticipate many of his needs and be the best parent possible for him.

Chapter 10
Encouraging Words

As you've seen, just like parenting your children, there's a lot to be done in parenting your dog. It's a full-time undertaking. However, it's not as hard to be a good parent for your dog as it may sometimes seem. What does it take to be a good parent who has a well-behaved dog? It takes a normal, average person willing to accept responsibility for being a good leader, just like with your other kids. There's no magic involved in being a good parent for your dog or your kids. If you're capable of having good kids, you're capable of having good dogs because the same parenting skills are involved with raising either one. Everyone wants to be a good parent, and everyone can be. Problems will naturally arise during your parenting, but if you've got the savvy and the desire for parenting, you can cope with just about anything.

Remember Kitten, the St. Bernard who was aggressive around people? After she had graduated from the Academy she was a well-behaved dog. Even so, we still had a few doubts about how she would handle unusual situations involving new people. That was one of the reasons why Kitten was escorted to the big coming-out party. Kitten was a big hit at the party, but we still wondered how she'd react toward strangers in the future, long after her training with us was over.

The behaviorist who had originally recommended Kitten's owners to us called and said she wanted Kitten to appear on a television show with her. Kitten's owners agreed, provided we accompany Kitten on the show. So, we ended up escorting Kitten to the television studio.

The filming of a television program is absolutely chaotic. There are cables and huge spotlights and strange noises and people coming and going shouting at one another and wearing funny looking headsets. It's a real exercise in organized confusion. Kitten took all of this like a rock, but, like all St. Bernards, she drools like a waterfall. So, here comes a strange technician who's literally bristling with electronic equipment. He's got a huge boom mike strapped on his shoulder and earphones and wires and all this other stuff hanging off his arms and clothes. He marches right up to Kitten with a handkerchief in his hand and bends down slightly—Kitten's head is almost up to his chest—and just wipes that slobber right off her face! While this was going on, we were sitting in the studio audience ready to leap out of our seats to save the technician's life as he approached Kitten. Our fears were unfounded. Kitten quietly assented to having her muzzle wiped by this bizarre looking stranger, and we both sank down in our seats relieved.

This was the dog that only months earlier was almost entirely uncontrollable and who would have taken that guy's arm off if he had tried a similar stunt then. Kitten had changed. She hadn't had television training any more than she had had party training, but it didn't matter. Kitten had thoroughly mastered basic obedience commands that had been generalized to accommodate unanticipated situations. Kitten's owners now thought of Kitten as a completely different dog. Our training and their parenting skills had made a tough situation into one that was thoroughly satisfying and pleasurable for everyone involved. Kitten and her parents could look forward to many happy years together.

Parenting is the art of being a good leader. If you're not the leader your kids and your dogs are going to give you trouble. Again, though, being a good leader doesn't mean you have to be a drill sergeant to win respect and obedience. Being a good leader is about communicating your wishes clearly, accepting responsibility for enforcing good behavior, and being constant and consistent in your insistence on good behavior. If you can do that you can be a good parent for both your kids and your dogs.

Remember Attila? His first owner apparently couldn't or wouldn't accept that leadership role. As a result, Attila had to assume that responsibility himself to have a true working pack. Attila was in charge and, as far as he was concerned, he wasn't going allow any nonsense.

This was a big responsibility for Attila, and one he didn't seem to be temperamentally prepared for. But, to his way of thinking, *somebody* had to be in charge or the pack was going to fall apart. Perhaps against his own inclination, he assumed that responsibility for the welfare of the pack. When Attila finally got matched up with a real *alpha*, he could relax and be happy again. Everything was fine, because he had a pack leader— a parent—who was looking out for him and who could relieve the heavy burden of having to run things. When Attila found someone who was willing to be a leader and a parent, every-

Perfect Partners

thing went well for the pack. Having a happy pack requires you to be its leader. If you can do that, you'll be happy. You'll have kids and dogs who know where they stand, who know what's expected of them, and who know that someone is always looking out for them. When that happens, you can expect obedience from your dogs and your kids.

The joys of parenting are many, and there's nothing that can substitute the kind of satisfaction that comes from being a parent. There's nothing like hearing someone say to you: "Boy, you sure have great kids," or, "Boy, you sure have a nice dog." You can have both. All you need to do is be a good parent. Anyone can do it. We hope this book will help make it a little easier.

Index

Abstract command 69
Adulthood 27
Aggression 109,142
Ailments, breed-related 147
Allergy 141
Alpha 15, 35, 47, 62
Alpha female 11
Alpha male 11
American Kennel Club 85, 134
Anxiety, food 142
Assertiveness 119
Australian Cattle Dog 122
Australian Shepherd 123
Authority 35, 43
Bark 81
Basic Training 57
Basset Hound 143
Beagle 82, 94
Bearing 44
Behavior, change in 109
Behavior, conditioned 77
Behavior, emerging 111
Behavior, negative 70, 114, 119
Behavior, pack 4, 9, 110
Behavior, unwanted 110
Behavioral problems 127
Behaviors, learned 3
Benefits 51
Beta 15
Bite, inhibited 19

Body language 44, 84
Border Collie 123
Bottle, squirt 82
Boxer 110, 114
Breed of dog 119
Brittany Spaniel 143
Brush, rake 159
Brush, slicker 159
Bulldog 147
Bumpers 163
Challenges 111
Change 28, 48, 116, 119
Childbirth 27, 48
Chow Chow 44, 147
Clippers, toenail 160
Cocker Spaniel 22, 111
Collar 152
Collar, choke-chain 79, 152
Collar, link-chain 79
Collar, pinch 153
Collar, training 79, 152
Come 68, 91
Command types 69
Commands, abstract 76
Communicate 29, 33
Concrete command 69
Conditioned command 69
Conformation ring 135
Consequences 51
Consistency 45, 62, 83, 109
Constancy 51, 109

Coordination 18
Correction 46, 47, 77-79, 153
Crate 156
Decision, incorrect 78
Development 26, 29
Diet 141
Discipline 13
Distractions 65
Divorce 27, 48
Dog, nice 168
Dominance 46, 48, 80
Domination games 18
Don't pull 68
Down 44, 66, 85
Down/Stay 67, 87
Drop 85
Dysplasia, hip 143
Earache 143
Ears, drooping 144
Energy 22
Eyesight 143
Fear 23, 46, 129
Fear Imprint Stage 19, 21, 81
Food anxiety 142
Freeze-state 71
Generalization 54, 56, 59, 65, 83, 85, 88
German Shepherd 143, 159, 160
Get home 68
Get/Go on/Go away 68
Go to rug 67
Golden Retriever 28, 80
Great Dane 22,29, 80, 136
Grooming 160
Grooming tools 159
Groundrules 54
Habit, creatures of 55
Habits 96
Hand signal 84
Health 143
Help, professional 109
High-energy dog 120

Hormones 25
Housetraining 95-100
Hunting breeds 120
Husky 159
Identification methods 154
Infection, bladder 144
Instinctive 3
Irish Water Spaniel 76
Jack Russell Terrier 29
Kisses 77
Labrador, Black 138
Lady and the Tramp Syndrome 130
Leader of the pack 35
Leaders 15, 40
Leadership 14, 46, 51, 106, 109, 114
Learned behaviors 3
Leash 153
Leave it 67, 89
Life expectancy 147
Lifestyle 120
Littermates 18
Malamute 159
Marking 95
Marriage 48
Matting 160
Maturation rate 22
Mature mentally, how dogs 17
Mature physically, how dogs 17
Mid-life crisis 27, 29
Miniature Pinscher 80
Moving 27
Negative behavior 25, 106
Nervous system, puppy's 17
Neuter 26, 131
Newfoundland 131
Noisemakers 81
Nurturing 128
Nutrition 142
Obedience 53, 63, 65, 78, 106, 109
Off 68

Old age 29
Omega 16
Pack 48
Pack behavior 4, 9, 110
Pack dynamics 110, 114
Pack leader 65, 77, 137
Pack structure 12
Pain tolerance 127
Parenting 5, 106, 137, 151, 165
Pavlov, Ivan 69
Pens, exercise 157
Pets, throw-away 7
Play, initiates 16
Play bow 16
Pomeranian 41, 136
Poodle 136
Portuguese Water Dog 147
Possession 18
Posture 44
Posturing 16
Praise 90
Pregnancy, false 134
Protection dog 126
Puberty 22
Punishment 78
Puppy, newborn 17
Puppy Private 21, 92
Quiet 67, 81
Rawhide 163
Respect 35
Responsibilities 33
Reverse Chaining 92
Ring, dead 79
Ring, live 79
Ritual 55
Rottweiler 27, 55, 117, 142
Routine 55,
Rug 158
Schedule 97
Sensitive 29
Separation 27
Shar-Pei 44, 147

Shelter, animal 6
Signal, hand 84
Sit 66, 73, 83
Socialization 9, 19, 21
Spay 26, 131, 133
Springer Rage 144
Springer Spaniel 143
St. Bernard 58
Stay 66, 87, 89
Stimuli, positive 70
Storage disease 147
Stripper 159
Structure 51, 109
Submission response 15
Supervise 98
Temperament 23, 122
Territory 53
Testosterone 132
Threat, empty 40
Threat 40
Thyroid condition 146
Throw-away pets 7
Time 84, 88
Toenail clippers 160
Tools, grooming 159
Toys 162
Toys, chew 162
Toys, squeaky 163
Trainer, professional 105
Training 52, 65, 83, 92, 105
Trauma 28
Trust 45
Vaginitis 144
Veterinarian 143
Vocabulary, concrete 72
Vocabulary, conditioned 72
Vocabulary, training 65
Vocalizations 16
Voice, tone of 44
Wait 66, 89